Praise for *The Path of the Genie*

There are inspirational books and there are inspirational books…but none has so totally captured my interest until this superb book by Dr. Dilip. He takes you on a magical journey using the familiar story of Aladdin, the Genie, and the three wishes. I especially liked what Dr. Dilip says early in his book, "Dust off your spirit" as I am a firm believer in keeping one's spirit alive and fulfilled. You will enjoy this easy to read book that jolts you into the realization of life's promises if one just looks at oneself with "new eyes" and follows Dr. Dilip's "Path of the Genie." Thanks for an easy to read, straightforward book that can renew one's spirit.

**—Theodore Charles Wood, Past International President,
Toastmasters International**

Finally there is a book that takes you so deep it speaks to your spirit. *The Path of the Genie* guides you on a tremendous journey of fulfillment and joy. It is not just a book, it is a life-changing tool. I couldn't put it down, so I didn't. Dilip Abayasekara has written a book destined to be of great importance to countless readers. Everyone can benefit immensely from understanding and following *The Path of the Genie*. I know I have.

**—Craig Valentine,
1999 World Champion of Public Speaking**

This book helps us to pause, ponder, and respond to that inner voice which calls us to be "the person we ought to be." Dilip Abayasekara writes as he lives, a life full of meaning and fulfillment. Make sure you read this. His insight will inspire you.

**—Priyan Fernando, Executive Vice President & Chief
Operating Officer, Global Corporate Travel,
American Express Company.**

Throughout one's life there are occasions when we question our priorities. *The Path of the Genie* offers clear guidance with supportive references that helped me understand what truly is important and showed me how to get there. Thank you, Dr. Dilip, for compiling and sharing your wisdom. Your gift allows many others to find direction and meaning for their lives. Together, we will improve our world.

**—Todd A. Milano, President,
Central Pennsylvania College**

Dr. Abayasekara's book, *The Path of the Genie*, makes clear that the path to fulfillment is not an ego trip; it is a path full of appreciation for others, for the world, and for oneself. The Path of the Genie is a practical, do-able, journey. The prose is marked by brisk, clean, insightful writing. The marvelous selection of quotes represents a rich cross-cultural heritage that taps into people in a wide range of cultures. He is well qualified to teach us about our paths to fulfillment through the wide lens of his approach to life. This book speaks usefully to the towering possibilities within the grasp of every human being.

**—Neil L. Irons, Bishop,
United Methodist Church**

Wow, your words are sincere, soothing, and inspiring. Thanks for putting me back on track. You've convinced me to "dust off my spirit!" Thank you—everyone should read this. If you are not feeling fulfilled, *The Path of the Genie* is a must read. Dr. Dilip, your words and experiences are truly inspiring and thought provoking. Thank you.

**—Darren LaCroix,
2001 World Champion of Public Speaking**

Dr. Dilip clearly lays out solid principles for living a meaningful, rewarding, and fulfilling life. In clear, concise, and conversational fashion, he draws from personal experience and the wisdom of the ages as he guides his readers along The Path of the Genie. His practical action steps are powerful tools, which will catapult those who take them to a new level of self-discovery and fulfillment. Enjoy the journey!

—**Mark L. Brown,**
1995 World Champion of Public Speaking

As I read *The Path of the Genie*, the words from a song in the movie *Aladdin* rang in my ears—"A whole new world ... A new fantastic point of view ... A dazzling place I never knew ... But when I'm way up here, it's crystal clear ..." Dilip has provided us a magic carpet ride—a crystal clear path to our heart's desire, and it opens up a whole new and wonderful world. It is amazing how many new and wonderful things we can learn from children's stories. Dilip has done more than Disney could have in providing us with the eternal truths in Aladdin's story. Dilip has kept his message simple, timely, and relevant. And yet, the far-reaching implications of "The Path" will help everyone find themselves, find meaning in their lives, and find fulfillment in all that they endeavor. Truly a "must read!"

—**Johnny "Pawe" T. Uy, Chairman and CEO,**
Pawe Group of Companies, Cebu City, Philippines

The need for self-fulfillment is a fundamental motivational force within every human being. When understood and acted upon, it becomes the primary driving factor in defining who we are. Dilip Abayasekara brilliantly uses personal experiences and perfectly chosen examples to illustrate the importance of identifying one's own self-fulfillment driver. Equally as important, he provides easy to follow action steps for the journey. *The Path of the Genie* is interesting, extremely well-written, practical, and powerful. It is a must-read for those who believe they have achieved success and for those still on the journey.

—**Eddie Vincent Dunn, Vice Chancellor for Strategic**
Planning and Executive Director of the College Technical
Education Council, North Dakota University System and
Past International President, Toastmasters International.

Hopefully, this excellent little self-help book will give you the courage "to discover your bottled up music" and allow you to find fulfillment regardless of your stage in life. Young and old can benefit from this inspirational story.

—**Patricia H. Vance, State Representative,**
87th District, Pennsylvania, USA

The Path of the Genie has an immediacy that makes it magical ... Dr. Dilip R. Abayasekara has a generous heart, and an honest one. The Path of the Genie is an informed and magical perspective for those who have been soul searching for a clear-sighted road map to their heart's desire. It's a MUST read that you will find moving, inspiring, life altering, and effective. This book has such genuine and caring power that you will find yourself reading *The Path of the Genie* again and again!

—**Ty Howard, Chairman & CEO,**
The Baltimore Worldwide Speakers Bureau

The Path of the Genie challenges you to look at the magic within yourself and seek the path of fulfillment. Dr. Dilip Abayasekara provides a road map to rediscover your life and set a course towards reaching your heart's desire.

—**Jay R. Murray, Senior Vice President and Chief Operating Officer, Mid-Atlantic Federal Credit Union**

There are myriads of books on self-help, and there are just as many on faith. Dilip has combined the two with a very touching personal story. Yes, he's a Christian. It's a Christian journey. You just might want to take it.

—**Clifford L. Jones, Former Secretary,**
Pennsylvania Department of Labor and Industry

Dr. Dilip Abayasekara has outlined a technique for self-discovery—a method to live life in fullness. We each have a gift. The "Genie" within each of us can help us to discover our unique talent and become the person we want to be. *The Path of the Genie* leads the readers to discover their own genius and path of fulfillment. Join in this walk with Dr. Dilip. It will make a difference in your life. One of my favorite children's books is *The Little Engine That Could*. Dr. Dilip Abayasekara's book, *The Path of the Genie*, in a refreshing and fun way, outlines how we can succeed just as the little engine did. The Genie helps us to discover our gifts, reach fulfillment, and become the person we want to be. And "Yes," we can make it over the mountain.

**—William R. Ecker, President/CEO,
Bill Ecker Enterprises**

The difference between happiness and fulfillment may seem superficial, but the chasm between the two is vast. In *The Path of the Genie*, Dilip Abayasekara explains the difference and shows us how we can use Aladdin's journey to fulfillment as a guide for our own voyage of discovery. All you need to embark on that voyage are an open mind, a willing spirit, and an understanding heart.

—David Brooks, 1990 World Champion of Public Speaking

This book was well conceived and well written. *The Path of the Genie* sheds a bright light on how to live a happy and productive life. I re-read several chapters in order to be sure to implement their profound principles. Dilip, thank you for sharing your ideas and your life.

**—Philip P. Monetti,
Partner, The Integrity Group**

Dr. Abayasekara blends his career experiences, the story of Aladdin, Biblical events, historic figures, and a touch of American folklore into a compelling essay on the pursuit of personal fulfillment. This book reveals the need for humility, integrity, and charitable giving in pursuit of your heart's desire. A must read for those interested in expanding their vision of life.

—John S. Latin, Past International President, Toastmasters International

In Dilip's conversational style, he reaches out to touch both the mind and the heart. Step by step through the book he also gives you specifics on taking action in your own life. Dilip encourages each of us to live differently—to live lives of impact and integrity.

—Don Schin, Entrepreneur & Speaker
President, Pennsylvania Region, ACTION International

I have found *The Path of the Genie: Your Journey to Your Heart's Desire* a truly inspiring publication. What is uniquely impressive about the work is the bringing together, within a coherent framework, of intensely personal experiences, each of which has immediate relevance to life's travails and challenges. Particularly powerful are the passages relating to self-discovery and a sense of mission or purpose. The book cannot but make a profound impression on any perceptive reader.

—Professor G.L. Peiris, Member of Parliament
Former Minister of Constitutional Affairs, Sri Lanka

Both the casual reader and the professional will benefit from *The Path of the Genie*. The text draws upon popular and classical literature, the arts, and story in motivating an inward journey that leads to outward manifestations of values and meaningful life. Dr. Abayasekara is to be commended for helping others find their "center" and fulfill their desire to grow and serve.

—Rev. Dr. George Edwin Zeiders
President, Union Theological Seminary, Dayton, Ohio

The ease with which Dilip makes use of Aladdin's life to symbolize our own takes us back to the time when we were asking deep questions; questions which may have not yet been answered. And, as we have dreamt, we can use the very same path as Aladdin in order to discover who we are and what we want from life, just as Aladdin. The author uses three wishes to commence a path for the reader's self-discovery: the wish for humility, the wish for self-discovery, and finally the wish for self-offering. Dilip must be toasted for the simplicity with which he has addressed the significant complexities of life. This book is recommended reading for someone who wants to solve the answers to their life questions. It can be read alone, or even with your children if you wish to give them a head start in life, which is what I did, reading it with my daughter.

—Kumar Nadesan
CEO, Express Newspapers (Ceylon) Ltd.
Colombo, Sri Lanka

Transformation is the order of the world today. *The Path of the Genie* talks of the total transformation of an individual. Unlike any other self-development books, Dr. Dilip Abayasekara takes us through a step-by-step practical approach towards fulfilling our heart's desire. On the whole, as a true Toastmaster, I was so proud and pleased to read the book. This book is a God-given gift to any individual who aspires to live a life with a sense of purpose and fulfillment.

—Arunasalam Balraj
CEO, The Gemtrans Engineering Co.
Head, Territorial Council of South Asia for
Toastmasters International in Sri Lanka

The Path of the Genie
Your Journey to Your Heart's Desire

Dilip R. Abayasekara, Ph.D.

Executive Books

The Path of the Genie:
Your Journey to Your Heart's Desire

Published by
Executive Books
206 West Allen Street
Mechanicsburg, PA 17055
717-766-9499 800-233-2665
Fax: 717-766-6565
www.ExecutiveBooks.com

Copyright © 2004 by Dilip R. Abayasekara

Teflon® is a registered trademark of E.I. duPont deNemours and Company.

ISBN: 0-937539-05-8

Printed in the United States of America

DEDICATION

This book is dedicated to the most important
people in my life. They have stood by me,
supported me, and believed in me…and still do–
My wife Sharon, our children Allison & Alexander,
my parents Earle & Anne Abayasekara, and
my brothers and sisters and their spouses:
Ranmali & Ajit, Rohan & Suvendrini, Ranjan & Niranjala, Sarla & Chandran,
Ranil & Charmalie, and Anusha & Shantilal.
Thank you for nourishing the music within me.
May your sweet music always be heard.

CONTENTS

ACKNOWLEDGEMENTS

A s *The Path of the Genie* shows, this message has arisen because many people aided, guided, and inspired me. I owe them a debt of gratitude that I cannot repay. While space limitations do not allow me to list the name of every individual who has helped me discover my path, I do want to acknowledge a few who stand out as Genies in my life.

My wife Sharon has been a magnificent and faithful friend and supporter, nourishing my dreams. My children, Allison and Alex, invited me to watch a movie that gave rise to the heart of this message. Furthermore, Allison was an invaluable help with editing. My brother Ranjan and his wife Niranjala gave me financial support at a very difficult time in my speaking career. My former Mastermind buddies and fellow professional speakers, Bill Ecker and Michael Hudson, encouraged me greatly in my formative years as a professional speaker. Longtime friend Tony Maxwell, who discovered his own path, has been a consistent encourager for me to complete this book. Jo Condrill, valued friend, Toastmaster, and encourager, led the way by writing her first book while I was still only dreaming of mine.

Todd Milano, President of Central Pennsylvania College, recognized my strengths, gave me opportunities to exercise them, and has been a positive presence in my professional life. David Brooks, Toastmasters 1990 World Champion of Public Speaking, taught me a great deal when he mentored me, encouraged me, and consoled me in the ups and downs of speech contests many years ago. Will Johnson, Toastmasters 1981 World Champion of Public Speaking, graciously shared his expertise with me as did Don Johnson, Toastmasters 1989 World Champion of Public Speaking. My professional speech coach Lila Alson taught me how to modify my accent so that Americans could understand my speech more easily.

Many thanks are due to Jason Liller of Executive books who directed and oversaw the publication of this book, answered my numerous questions, attended to editorial corrections and changes, and maintained his cheerful and positive demeanor throughout the entire process. David Bullock of Susquehanna Direct designed a cover that is more beautiful and appropriate than I could have imagined. I received valuable editorial help from Allison Abayasekara, Sharon Abayasekara, Mark Brown, David Brooks, Phil Monetti, Linda Buffington, Todd Milano, Neil Irons, Patricia Vance, Cliff Jones, and Eddie Dunn. Anne Abayasekara supplied the story about self-offering in Sri Lanka.

In the past few years, Charlie "Tremendous" Jones has become a great mentor, inspiration, and role model for me. Charlie is a living testimony to how a transformed life can be a powerful force for good in this world. Last but certainly not least, my parents, Earle and Anne Abayasekara, nurtured me, sacrificed for me, encouraged me, and gave me the freedom to discover my own path. Thank you.

FOREWORD

Carlisle said, "If you are going to reach the heart, you must speak from the heart." Dr. Dilip Abayasekara, or "Dr. Dilip," as he is known to many, touched my heart very deeply with the message of this book. One thing will become abundantly clear to you as you read this book: Dilip has poured his heart into it and stirred it up with tremendous wisdom, humor, insight, and stories so that its words leap out at you with the power of authenticity.

I count myself among the many people who did not know, in my early years, in which direction I should take my life. If I had had the opportunity to read this book as a teenager or as a young man and put its principles in to practice, I know that I could have avoided many a heartache. Experience has taught me that happiness, fulfillment, and all the attendant "wants" of life are secondary to spiritual rebirth and growth. In this book, my friend Dilip unveils in a disarmingly straightforward, easy-to-read, but elegant manner, powerful principles that I believe will help anyone travel the path to their desired destination.

As I always say, five years from now you will be the same person you are today, except for two things: the people you meet, and the books you read. The next best thing to hearing Dilip speak is to read this book. I strongly commend its life-changing message.

Tremendously Yours,
Charlie "Tremendous" Jones

PREFACE

You are not an accident of nature. There is purpose and meaning behind your life. The hard part is finding that purpose and meaning. The path to finding your purpose and living out your destiny is what I call The Path of the Genie. In this book, I attempt to share with you what I have discovered to be guiding truths that will keep you and me on track.

The message that I share has been wrought from the fruits of my experience. That journey has literally changed my life. As you discover and travel your own path of the Genie, you will find that although your path has its own unique twists and turns, the guiding principles are the same. They can give new meaning, new power, and new purpose to you.

I do not pretend to have all the answers or the whole truth. What you will find here are practical guides, regardless of your particular faith or creed, which I believe can guide you to claim and live out your destiny. That is the journey to your heart's desire. That is the path to fulfillment.

Dilip R. Abayasekara

PART I

ENTER THE PATH

"You can't shake hands with your neighbor until you
drop the stone that is in your own hand."

– Dilip Abayasekara

YOUR HEART'S DESIRE

What is your heart's desire? How can you achieve your heart's desire? Why is your heart's desire so important to you?

After delivering a keynote speech to several hundred business professionals in a hotel ballroom, I was enjoying chatting with individual members of the audience when a young woman asked to speak to me privately. We withdrew to a quiet corner of the ballroom. She appeared to be in her early thirties. Her face had a transparent sincerity that was attractive, and her eyes focused on me with great earnestness.

"I was deeply touched about what you said about listening to the Genie within," she said. "I don't think the job I've been doing is the right one for me. I really want to find what I was meant to do, and then do it."

That young lady was echoing a universal cry to find one's heart's desire. I understood how she felt. Some time ago, I too had cried out that refrain. I had been at that dead end of life's road where I realized with sickening frustration that I was only spinning my wheels and not progressing anywhere meaningful for me. This cry articulates your desire for significance and fulfillment.

Regardless of what exactly a person wants, *everyone wants to be fulfilled*. Think about it. The guy who dreams about owning the corner gas station thinks that doing so will make him feel fulfilled. The young woman who wants to be independent and have a successful career believes that will bring her fulfillment. The young man who earnestly desires to become rich thinks that wealth will give him what he wants out of life.

We usually want several things in life. For an ambitious girl about to enter college, it might be to excel in her academics, make good friends at college, and get her own car. For a middle-aged man, it might be to increase his earnings so that he can pay off his debts, fund his children's college education, and save more for retirement. What are your dreams? Whatever they are, you believe that when you achieve them, you will have peace of mind...that you will feel fulfilled.

> **I believe that fulfillment goes down much deeper than happiness; it's the difference between the roots of a giant oak tree and the roots of the grass in your lawn.**

What I am about to share with you is a simple, but powerful approach to help you find your heart's desire and achieve it. As you practice it daily, it will give you a *deeper* appreciation for what *really* matters in life. It will challenge you to redefine what you mean by fulfillment. Notice that I didn't discuss "happiness." I believe that fulfillment goes down much deeper than happiness; it's the difference between the roots of a giant oak tree and the roots of the grass in your lawn.

When you are fulfilled, you feel a deep contentment. Fulfillment is a by-product of the choices you make and the life you choose to live. The question is, how do you make the right choices so that you live the kind of life that leads to contentment? That's the point of this book.

AN OLD STORY WITH ETERNAL TRUTHS

I found basic, but significant answers to the questions about achieving your heart's desire when I was watching a movie with my children, who were at that time in elementary school. The movie was about a young man who found himself in a cave. It was no ordinary cave, but instead, a cave of wonders. The cave was filled with an enormous amount of material wealth. Rubies, emeralds, and diamonds glittered in the dim light. Golden goblets, silver vases, and statues studded with precious stones were all around him. Gold coins worth a king's ransom were overflowing from large chests! However, the young man had a problem. He was trapped in that cave; there was no way out.

As this youth looked around that cave, he spied something that looked out of place. It was a dusty old lamp. Curiously, he brushed the dirt and grime off the lamp. Suddenly, a vapor poured out of the spout of the lamp, and there appeared a magnificent looking Genie! The Genie granted the young man three wishes that changed his life forever. You probably have guessed whom I'm talking about. Yes, it was Aladdin.

This story may be old, but embedded in it are secrets that can change your life. Those secrets can lead you to your own fulfilled life. The journey that Aladdin took with his Genie is what I call *"The Path of the Genie."* This path is not Aladdin's alone. It belongs to every person who achieves his or her heart's desire. It can be your path. To discover the secrets of Aladdin's journey to his heart's desire, you need only three things: an open mind, an understanding heart, and a willing spirit. Are you ready? If so, let's proceed.

FIRST, DUST OFF YOUR SPIRIT

The Path of the Genie does not start with a wish. For Aladdin, it began when he wiped the dust and grime off the lamp. It was that cleansing action that triggered the release of the Genie who had been trapped in that lamp for a very long time. Think about it. The lamp represents your spirit. The Genie represents your inner voice, the divinity that exists within each person.

The reason that we don't hear that "still, small voice" is because the dust and grime of life dulls our spirit. The dust and grime are the negative attitudes that we store up as we traverse our path of life. Just as dirt and dust dull the shine of a lamp, a myriad of negatives such as bitterness, hate, jealousy, envy, self-pity, and arrogance will dull the shine of your spirit. When that happens, you don't hear the whispers of your inner voice, your Genie remains trapped, and there is no way out of your cave.

The first step on The Path of the Genie is clear. It is to jettison the negatives that hold you back. You can't move forward easily when your spirit is burdened. It's similar to a situation I encountered with my car. One morning I got into my car, turned the ignition key, and nudged the gas pedal. But the car was sluggish in its movement forward. Then I realized that I had forgotten to release the emergency brake. The moment I released the brake, the car moved easily and freely. When you let go of those "brakes," the negatives in your life, you can move forward … and hear the voice of your genie.

NEW EYES

There is an old and very insightful saying that goes, "If you want the world to change, look at the world with new eyes." In a sense, you and I don't really see the world as it is. In much the same way that negative attitudes dull your

> **No one has ever died from a snakebite. It's the venom circulating in the blood that kills!**
> **—Craig Valentine**

spirit, negative feelings cloud your view of the world. Feelings such as anger, fear, cynicism, and despair act like cataracts on the eye. When you let go of these negative feelings, the "cataract" is removed and you see clearly. The world looks quite different!

In June 1999 I heard a riveting speech by Craig Valentine, who later went on to become Toastmasters 1999 World Champion of Public Speaking. Craig's speech was titled "Snake Bite." Craig began the speech by claiming that no one has ever died from the bite of a snake. Noting our puzzled expressions, Craig went on to make his case by saying that it is not the bite itself that is fatal but that it is the venom circulating in the bloodstream that kills! Craig's point was that hate, prejudice, and grudges we hold against others are like the poison of snake venom circulating in our spirits. The act of forgiveness is an act that cleanses you and is a vital step to your inner healing. When you forgive, you dust off your spirit. The lamp begins to shine, and your own Genie appears.

FIVE ACTION STEPS TO SHINE YOUR LAMP

1. **Write a letter to God.** This idea comes from the book *I'm Rich Beyond My Wildest Dreams,* by Thomas L. Pauley and Penelope J. Pauley. If you are full of anger or hate or envy or any other negative emotion and find it difficult to let it go, write a letter to God about how you feel. Pour out your feelings. Be honest. Ask for help. Then destroy the letter or put it away. You will feel like a burden has been lifted from your shoulders.

2. **Imagine healing.** In your mind's eye, see yourself making peace with the person with whom you have strained relations. Hear yourself say words of affection and forgiveness to that person. Feel the release of tension and the inflowing of peace. What you regularly imagine vividly will become your reality.

3. **Let it be.** Listen to the Beatles' song, *Let it be.*

4. **Do something good for others.** Help someone who can't repay you or return the favor. Volunteer your time in a soup kitchen or crisis center, a hospital, nursing home, or Boys and Girls Club. You will find you forget (release) your own hurt as you become engrossed in helping others.

5. **Ask for forgiveness.** Even if someone else is at fault for hurting you and straining your relationship, you will find release and peace of mind if you ask that person to forgive you for the negative thoughts that you have been harboring.

PART II

THE FIRST WISH

"The doorstep to the temple of wisdom is the knowledge of one's own ignorance."

– Charles Spurgeon

GETTING OUT OF YOUR CAVE

Aladdin's first wish was to get out of that cave. Did he do that on his own power? No. He relied on the power of the Genie to help him escape from the cave. This reveals several things about Aladdin's outlook. First, Aladdin realized that he needed help. Second, he recognized the Genie as someone who could help him. Third, he tapped the power of the Genie to help him get out of the cave. This behavior can be summed up as the wish for humility.

The meaning often associated with the word "humility" is not flattering. It is derived from the Latin *humilitas* signifying a lowly state or submission. However, I use the word here in an entirely different context.

The "wish for humility" begins with recognizing that you need the help of other people to achieve whatever you want in life. It is a proclamation that we are interdependent beings. It is another way of joining the poet John Donne in saying, "No man is an island entire of itself. Every man is a piece of the continent, a part of the main."

Humility can't be forced on a person, nor can one bargain for humility. This is illustrated by the story about a couple at their church altar. The man prayed earnestly, "Dear Lord, please make me successful; I promise I'll be humble." Overhearing her husband's prayer, the wife said, "Dear Lord, YOU make him successful; I'll keep him humble!"

No. Humility is not a bargaining chip. It is the first step

in learning to tap the riches around you. Humility allows you to recognize that others around you have strengths that you don't have. Humility enables you to appreciate others, listen to them, and learn from them. Author Harvey Mackay expresses it like this in one of his 'Mackay's Maxims': "No matter how smart you are, no matter how talented, you can't do it alone."

Sometimes, when you try to avoid humility, you can be humbled. I discovered the truth of that soon after I came to the USA at the age of 19. I was born and raised in Sri Lanka, the tropical island off the southern tip of India. Sri Lanka is culturally very different from the States. Soon after I arrived, I spent a wonderful two weeks as the guest of the Kirsch family in Dayton, Ohio.

The first morning I sat down to breakfast with them, Mrs. Kirsch served me bacon, eggs, and toast. Before I came to the States, to prepare for my American experience, I had practiced eating with a knife and fork. But that morning in Dayton, I soon realized that I had not prepared myself for every contingency. I wanted to eat the toast, but was not sure whether it was acceptable to pick up the toast with my fingers or whether I should use the silverware. All I had to do was be humble and ask anyone at the table what I should do. But, I didn't want to ask anyone because I was afraid that they might laugh at me. I waited for a while for someone to eat their toast so that I could imitate them, but no one did. So I plunged ahead and started to cut up the toast. Upon seeing what I was doing, the eyes of the six-year old girl sitting across from me grew wide in astonishment. She exclaimed loudly, "Look Mom, he's eating the toast with his knife and fork!" You should have seen how fast I put down my silverware!

Why didn't I ask my hosts about the "proper" way to eat the toast? It was because I didn't want to show my ignorance. In trying to avoid humility, humility was thrust upon me.

Charles Spurgeon said, "The doorstep to the temple of wisdom is the knowledge of one's own ignorance." It is that self-knowledge that prompts you to seek the help of those who can help you.

> **In trying to avoid humility, humility was thrust upon me.**

THREE QUESTIONS THAT ARISE FROM HUMILITY

There are three basic questions that arise from this spirit of humility when you are on the path of self-improvement:

What must I learn?

How can I improve?

Who can teach me?

The yearning for learning is an expression of humility. It is said that as a young man, Abraham Lincoln would think nothing of walking 20 miles to hear accomplished speakers and learn from them. Soon after the American Civil War started, President Lincoln realized the tremendous odds he faced. His humble words still ring down the passage of time, touching a nerve that is common to us all, because any one of us who has been backed into an impossible situation could say the same: "I must confess that I am driven to my knees by the overwhelming conviction that I have nowhere else to go. My wisdom and that of all about me are insufficient to meet the demands of the day."

Consider another man who in later life played a decisive role in world history. When young soldier Winston Churchill was stationed in India, he realized that he wasn't as educated as many of his peers in the classics, economics, history, and the English language. He believed that he was called to be a leader and had the wisdom to know that a leader should be knowledgeable about his world, past and present. So he asked his mother, who was in England, to mail him books that would fill his knowledge gaps. He spent many a hot afternoon studying the works of Macaulay, Shakespeare, Milton, and the books of great philosophers and historians. They were his Genies.

Churchill was preparing himself for great leadership. Intuitively he knew that someday he would fulfill that call. Little did the world know that Churchill was destined to play a crucial role many years later in leading the free world against the tyranny of Hitler. Can you imagine the state the world would be in if Churchill had shown no desire to learn, improve, and grow?

Your sense of humility is also revealed by the respect you have for others. The person who lacks humility is not only arrogant, but frequently is cynical. Such a person can be described by the old saying, "A cynic is someone who knows the price of everything and the value of nothing."

Why is respect for others a reflection of your humility? Looking through the eyes of humility allows you to see how much others can teach you. Ralph Waldo Emerson captured this insight when he said, "Every man I meet is my superior in some way, in that, I can learn from him."

I recall a time when I was made aware that I needed to improve significantly as a speaker. It was 1992 and I had just won my Toastmasters District's speech contest that day. Quite naturally I felt on top of the world. Before leaving that conference hall, I ran into Ted Wood, a man I respect greatly, a past President of Toastmasters International. This gentleman had been a chief judge at Toastmasters World Championship of Public Speaking. His words to me were very different from the words of praise and acclamation that had been heaped on me by others. Ted, in his inimitable, subtle way, let me know that I was not as good a speaker as I thought I was!

He planted the thought in my mind that I needed to greatly improve if I wanted to win at the next level of the contest cycle, and he offered to give me pointers. With his words of advice fresh in my mind, I telephoned him a few days later. So began a learning process that played a vital role in taking me to the "next level" and achieving a long time goal of becoming a finalist at Toastmasters World Championship of Public Speaking. This happened not only once, but twice! While I will always be thankful to

Ted, I am very glad that my desire to improve was stronger than my pride.

The eyes of humility also lead you to respect others because you know that every person has inherent value.

A western reporter visited Mother Teresa in India. As they walked along the streets of Calcutta, Mother Teresa stopped by a wretched looking man who had leprous sores. With eyes full of compassion, she drew him to her, wrapping her arms around him in a warm embrace. The reporter gasped, "How can you do that? How can you even get close to … that?" Looking up from her kneeling position, Mother Teresa simply explained, "In everyone I see a child of God."

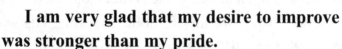

I am very glad that my desire to improve was stronger than my pride.

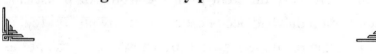

It often takes an extreme situation to turn around a person who rejects the attitude of humility. In an issue of the Parade Magazine, writer Dotson Rader reported an interview he had with the movie star Charlie Sheen. He told how, despite Sheen's successful acting career, he got hooked on drugs that threatened to destroy his life and his relationships. At the end of his rope, he was successful in undergoing rehabilitation at a residential drug treatment facility. Rader reported these words from Sheen: "I had a hole in me that got bigger and bigger the more I tried to fill it with people and expensive things and drugs. Then it was all stripped away, and I learned that you can't fill the hole that way. It has to be filled with something else—with faith and love and humility."

THE THREE Rs OF HUMILITY

It is one thing to be humble when you have reached the end of your rope. Perhaps a harder test of your humility is how you relate to others when you are at the top of your game. Your outer actions are a reflection of your inner understanding.

The person who practices humility is easy to spot. Just watch the way that he or she interacts with others. You will see the three Rs of humility: respect, regard, and recognition of interdependence. Philosopher, poet, literary and cultural critic George Santayana expressed it beautifully: "If a man be gracious and courteous to strangers, it shows that he is a citizen of the world, and that his heart is no island cut off from other lands, but a continent that joins them."

Read the eloquent call to environmental responsibility (often incorrectly attributed to Seattle, Chief of the Suquamish tribe) written by Ted Perry, a screenwriter who worked for the Southern Baptist Convention's Radio and Television Commission. Perry wrote it for *Home*, a 1972 film about ecology. "…This we know: the earth does not belong to man, man belongs to the earth. All things are connected like the blood that unites us all. Man did not weave the web of life; he is merely a strand in it. Whatever he does to the web, he does to himself." The dominant theme of this message is our interconnectedness with each other and with our universe.

Humility, in addition to recognizing your interconnectedness, also opens the door to recognizing your blessings. Here's a poignant poem sent to me by a friend, author unknown:

The little child whispered, "God, speak to me."
And a meadowlark sang, but the child did not hear.
So the child yelled, "God, speak to me!"
And the thunder rolled across the sky,
but the child did not listen.
The child looked around and said,
"God let me see you."
And a star shone brightly, but the child did not notice.
Then the child shouted, "God show me a miracle!"
And a life was born, but the child did not know.
So the child cried out in despair, "Touch me God,
And let me know you are here!"
Whereupon God reached down and touched the child.
But the child brushed the butterfly away
And walked away unknowingly.

When you practice the first wish of *The Path of the Genie*, you become aware—aware of the potential and greatness in others—aware of God's working in your life. Humility will open your eyes and give you the awareness to recognize your interconnectedness, which will quite naturally lead you to regard others with respect. It also will create a desire to learn and grow from others.

PARTNERSHIPS—THE PRACTICAL APPLICATION OF HUMILITY

Throughout the story of Aladdin's rise from street urchin to prince, the common thread is the partnership of Aladdin with the Genie. In the end, both the Genie and Aladdin attained their heart's desires because they individually were committed to help each other.

The business world has been moving in the direction of partnerships for many years. Hotel chains and restaurant chains frequently agree to locate next to each other so that they can share a common customer base. One business often carries an advertisement for another, non-competitive business and vice versa. In their websites, entrepreneurs often display links to related businesses. There are even books with titles such as *Stop Selling, Start Partnering* (by Larry Wilson with Hirsch Wilson, John Wiley & Sons) that inform and instruct you how to create win-win partnerships. The wish for humility is an essential step for the flowering of every successful partnership, whether it be your business or your marriage. Who would make a great partner to help you reach your heart's desire?

The wish for humility opens the door to awareness, learning, respect, self-improvement, and partnering with others. Just as Aladdin did with the Genie, it enables you to discover and nurture Genies in your life.

FIVE ACTION STEPS FOR CLAIMING THE WISH FOR HUMILITY

1. **Determine what guidance or expertise you need.** This depends on what you want to accomplish. Consider your goals, your current performance, where you fall short, and what knowledge, skills, or information you need.

2. **Recognize who can help you.** Ask, "Whom do I know who already has accomplished what I want to achieve?" Ask them for help. There also is a great deal of information available in books and on tapes. The Internet has become one of the greatest and most convenient sources of information.

3. **Listen.** Listen to others. In order to learn from an expert, you have to listen. But also listen to those with less expertise or experience than you. You can learn from almost everyone.

4. **Encourage.** Let someone who needs to hear it know that he or she is special. Acknowledge that every person has an intrinsic value.

5. **Form a mastermind group.** This is a group of people who meet on a regular basis to discuss matters of mutual interest with a focused goal of helping each other advance towards their objectives. The

Master Mind thus created, is greater than the sum of the individuals' mind power. This idea for self-advancement, using the combined wisdom and expertise of a small group of trusted people is described in the classic, *Think and Grow Rich*, written by Napoleon Hill, who spent a lifetime researching the secrets of success. You will find more information about the Master Mind principle in another of Napoleon Hill's books, *Magic Ladder to Success*, and in the book *Believe and Achieve—W. Clement Stone's 17 Principles of Success*, compiled by the Napoleon Hill Foundation.

PART III

THE SECOND WISH

"He is strong who conquers others; he who conquers himself is mighty."

– Lao-Tzu

FROM IMPOSTER TO AUTHENTIC SELF

The second wish on *The Path of the Genie* arises out of the quandary that Aladdin found himself in when he fell in love with beautiful Princess Jasmine. You may recall that Aladdin really was a poor boy living by his wits off the street. In order to win the hand of the princess, his second wish was to make himself look like a prince.

Although at first princess Jasmine rebuffs his advances, later she begins to show an interest in him. At this critical point, he could not be sure if she really loved him for who he was or if she loved the person he was pretending to be. Aladdin was caught in his own web of deception! Should he reveal to the princess who he really was or continue pretending to be someone he was not?

It is at this juncture that Aladdin points us to the second wish of the path of the Genie. It is the *wish for self-discovery*.

The granting of the wish for self-discovery leads you to know who you are. That's much easier said than done as shown by the saying, "To know yourself is the beginning of wisdom."

The problem is that facades often cover us up. It is like Russian toy dolls you may have seen. There is one very small, beautifully painted wooden doll within a slightly larger doll, which is within a still larger doll, which is within a larger doll, etc. Who you really are is the tiny doll in the heart of the doll package. To get to it, you have to open all the other dolls surrounding you. The person who surrounds himself with facades can soon forget his real identity.

SYMPTOMS OF LACK OF SELF-IDENTITY

When a person does not know who he really is, he often will try to adopt an identity that he thinks will please the people whose approval he seeks. Bruce Willis starred in a movie titled *The Kid*, which is a fable about a successful but unhappy image consultant who changes his life after being magically visited by himself as an 8-year old boy. In the movie, the boy assesses what Willis does, with these powerful, convicting words: "You help people lie about who they are, so they can pretend to be who they are not."

INTEGRITY—NO WORRIES
ABOUT THE FAMILY PARROT

A golfing couple had just returned home from a golf outing. They were putting their golf clubs away in the garage when the wife asked the husband, "Honey, if I were to die and you were to remarry, would you two live in our house?" The man paused for a moment and said, "It's paid for, so I guess so, dear." Frowning, his wife asked, "Would you let her drive my car?" This time, after only the slightest pause, the man replied, "Sure, why not?" Then she asked the really defining question, "Would you let her use my golf clubs?" Out tumbled the words, "Why no, she's left-handed." Truth will come out!

One reason to know who you really are is that it helps

you to live with integrity. Integrity is living in wholeness. What you think, what you say, what you do are all in sync. More important, when integrity is connected to your true self, and thereby to your purpose in life, you are able to live a life of power and meaning. That parallels something the cowboy philosopher Will Rogers said: "Live your life in such a manner that you wouldn't worry if the family parrot were sold to the town gossip!"

However guarded you are about your facades, at some-time or another you are going to slip up. Then, you will be found out! The only sure way to avoid that is to find out who you are, drop your masks, discover your gifts, use them to the fullest, and live a life that is whole. Then, there are no contradictory parts, because you are fully integrat-ed. When you live an integrated life, there is nothing to be "found out" but yourself. Just as Aladdin discovered, pri-vate demons of doubt will attack you even as you are pre-tending that everything is going just fine.

Fanny Brice expressed the meaning of this wholeness: "Let the world know you as you are, not as you think you should be. Sooner or later, if you are posing, you will for-get to pose, and then where are you?"

In 1934, the late author Dale Wimbrow wrote a great-ly admired but often misquoted poem. Sometimes it has been published with the title, "The Man in the Glass." Here it is as Wimbrow wrote it and published it in the *American Magazine*—a moving call to arms for integrity and wholeness. (Note that in the first line, "pelf" refers to money or riches.)

The Guy in the Glass

When you get what you want in the struggle for pelf,
And the world makes you king for a day,
Just go to the mirror and look at yourself,
And see what that guy has to say.

For it isn't your father, or mother, or wife,
Who judgment upon you must pass,
The feller whose verdict counts most in your life
Is the guy staring back from the glass.

He's the feller to please, never mind all the rest,
For he's with you clear up to the end.
And you've passed your most dangerous, difficult test
If the guy in the glass is your friend.

You may be like Jack Horner and "chisel" a plum,
And think you are a wonderful guy,
But the man in the glass says you're only a bum
If you can't look him straight in the eye.

You can fool the whole world down the pathway of years,
And get pats on the back as you pass,
But your final reward will be heartaches and tears
If you've cheated the guy in the glass.

© 1934 Dale Wimbrow

GET TO THE CENTER OF YOUR ONION

Sometimes when you are going through a personal crisis, you can gain insights about yourself. This happened to me when I was laid off from my job in 1989. I was a Senior Research Chemist for a large chemical company. Even though I knew that I could expect to lose my job, I didn't really know how I would feel when the ax fell. To my surprise, I felt both relief and pain—relief that I was leaving a bad job situation; pain that I had been rejected. Soon after the lay-off, when I was in my study silently trying to cope with this sense of rejection, I began to wonder who I was professionally. This led to a larger question: "Who am I?"

I drew a small circle and placed a question mark in the center of the circle. Then I drew a larger circle around that small circle. Then I drew still another circle around the two circles, and still another circle around that, as shown in the illustration below. Once I identified the outer layers, I went through the process of self-discovery by "peeling" each outer layer away, as if I were peeling away the layers of an onion.

Like the layers of an onion, you too have layers in your life. The layer that is closest to most of us is family. Then there is the layer of close friends, then occupation, then social acquaintances, etc. The order of the layers could be different for different people. Start by asking the question, "What layer of the onion represents my true identity?"

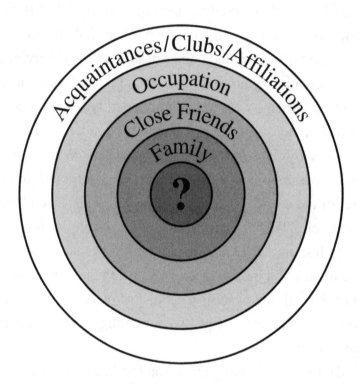

Onion Model of Self-identity

Do you think you are the family layer? If that is true, then if your family ceases to exist, you will cease to exist. So if your family is lost due to death or divorce or some tragedy, you will be lost. Do you think that you are your occupation? If that is true, then if your business goes bankrupt or if you are fired from your job, you will lose your identity. What if your sense of identity is wrapped up in your association with your friends? Then, if your friends reject you or if you move away from them, you will not be anyone, a nonentity. A sad reality of life is that we do lose families, mates, jobs, and friends. An even sadder reality is that some people lose their sense of self when they lose one or more of these layers.

WHO ARE YOU...REALLY?

You have to find out for yourself your real identity. You are more than your family, your mate, your job, your occupation, the organizations you belong to, or your friends. Your essence is that part that cannot be divorced, fired, or killed. Your essence is that part of the universe that was, that is, and that ever shall be. You are part of the continuum of life and energy and love.

For myself, I know that in the very center of that onion, I am a Child of God. This cannot be stripped from me. It is forever. What do I mean by the term "Child of God"? It means that I've accepted and committed to the Lordship of Jesus Christ in my life. With that commitment comes faith in the promises of God..."Who shall separate us from the love of Christ? Shall tribulation, or distress, or persecution, or famine, or nakedness, or peril, or sword? … But in all these things we are more than conquerors through Him who loved us. For I am convinced that neither death nor life, nor angels, nor principalities, nor things present, nor things to come, nor powers, nor height, nor depth, nor any other created thing, shall be able to separate us from the love of God which is in Christ Jesus our Lord." (Holy Bible, Romans 8: 35, 37-39, RSV).

You have to find out who you are for yourself. You must make your own discovery. Essentially, the second wish leads you to ask three questions:

"Who am I?"

"Am I becoming the person I ought to be?"

"What are my unique gifts?"

We have looked at the question "Who am I?" The second question, "Am I becoming the person I ought to be?" is a related and even more challenging one.

AM I BECOMING THE PERSON I OUGHT TO BE?

There is an old story about three blind men who came across an elephant. Each of the blind men felt the part of the elephant that was closest to him and described what the elephant must be like. The first blind man, feeling the elephant's tail, said, "This animal is like a rope." The second blind man, feeling the elephant's leg said "No. It's not like a rope. This animal is like a tree trunk." The third blind man, feeling the elephant's trunk exclaimed,

"You are both wrong. This animal is like a snake!"

Each man was right according to his perspective. But each man only was partially right. If they had sight, they would have seen the whole picture. We also can be very much like those blind men. In answer to the question, "Who am I?" you could say, "I am a mother." "I am a banker." "I am the president of so and so organization." Yet you will not have the full picture. It is only through spiritual insight that we are able to step back from what stares us in the face (the tail, the leg, the trunk) to understand our true nature (the whole elephant). When you do that, you discover the truth of what theologian Teilhard de

> **Don't be yourself. Be the person you ought to be.**
>
> **—Charles "T" Jones**

Chardin meant when he wrote, "We are not so much human beings on a spiritual journey as spiritual beings on a human journey."

What Teilhard de Chardin is saying is this—your authentic self is not your physical self. Your body is only a temporary casing in this earthly journey. You begin to discover the person you ought to be when you discover your spiritual self and your relation to the Creator. Becoming the person you ought to be is a spiritual journey that will last as long as you live. What matters is that you are making progress on this journey.

Self-discovery is important because it is when you

know who you really are, that you are able to fully live. You find the courage to cast off the facades that you have embraced or felt forced to accept. You discover the power to step forward, take risks, and live life with a sense of freedom and joy that is exhilarating. When Aladdin decided to tell Princess Jasmine who he really was, he made a decision to live authentically. That is a giant step toward personal freedom.

VALUES ARE A SNAPSHOT BUT NOT THE COMPLETE PICTURE

There was a time when I thought that a person's values are a good gauge to that person's identity. It seems logical, doesn't it? A murderer has values that are different from that of a law-abiding citizen. The flaw in that argument is that it does not take into account the fact that people change and therefore their values change. It does not mean that the person's identity changes. A person's values are only a snapshot in time of a changing person. Even the understanding a person has about a particular value can change with time.

TRANSFORMING AND BECOMING

I'm very fortunate to have as a friend and mentor, Charlie "Tremendous" Jones, the author of the best selling book *Life is Tremendous*. Charlie addresses this call for self-discovery when he says, "Don't be yourself. Be the person you ought to be."

Let's consider an imaginary story to illustrate these

principles of self-discovery: Mary and Joe have a son named Jim. Let's call this the primary identity. Baby Jim is kidnapped and raised as someone else's son. Does that mean that the primary identity changes? No! Jim will always be Mary and Joe's son, even though Jim may not be aware of it. Eventually boy Jim finds out that the people who are raising him had kidnapped him long ago and that his real parents are out there somewhere. Jim runs away and begins a search for his real parents. (*This can be likened to a person searching for his spiritual self.*) Finally, one day Jim locates his parents and finds out his primary identity. (*This is self-discovery.*) Now Jim begins a new life. He gets to know his parents more and more. He grows and discovers more about his roots and his possibilities. (*This is becoming the person he was meant to be.*)

To know yourself, you must search for truth, like Jim did in the above story. It is a spiritual quest. If you persist in the journey, it can transform you.

As I consider my own journey, I can see that my understanding of myself has changed significantly with time. I still espouse the values I held many years ago, but my understanding of what those values mean has entered a whole new dimension. Values such as love, kindness, and compassion have a new depth of meaning. Values that I previously didn't think deeply about such as servanthood and stewardship now challenge me to live in a certain way. This does not mean that my identity has changed. What it means is that I am becoming the person I ought to be. What's your story?

RESULTS OF TRANSFORMATION

Becoming who you are leads to a life of true freedom. One of the twentieth century's greatest freedom fighters was Mahatma Gandhi. As a young lawyer in South Africa, he experienced the dehumanizing cruelty of apartheid. This led to a transformation in his understanding of who he was and his calling in life. Returning to India, his native land, he saw a great people under the rule of a foreign power.

The attorney shed his law robes for the cotton cloth of a common man and grew into the unelected, but most influential Indian leader of his time. Gandhi discovered his unique gifts and his sense of self, which led to his sense of purpose and mission in life.

This story about Gandhi illustrates the congruity, the wholeness that characterizes a person's life when he knows who he is and is spiritually transformed. Before India was granted independence from the British, an American reporter was sent to India to write a story about Gandhi. He came upon Gandhi addressing a large public rally. The reporter noticed that Gandhi held the throng spellbound, hour after hour.

Finally, when Gandhi had finished, the reporter struggled through the crowd to talk to him, but the crush of bodies around Gandhi was too great for the reporter to get through. However, he was able to talk with Gandhi's secretary. "Tell me," he asked, "How does Gandhi keep the audience's attention for so long? He doesn't even use notes to speak. How does he do it?" The secretary thought for a moment, and then smiled and said, "I will tell you how. What the Mahatma thinks, how the Mahatma lives, what the Mahatma says, they are the same thing. He does not need notes!" The transformed person is a whole person. That is the story of Aladdin.

The Path of the Genie crosses all cultures and ethnicities. On the last day of the African-American celebration called Kwanzaa, the focus is on a time of assessment and self-reflection. It is a time to ask three Kwanzaa questions: Who am I? Am I really who I say I am? Am I all I ought to be? Aladdin had to go through such reflections to discover himself. It is part of *The Path of the Genie.*

TRANSFORMATION IS
DEPENDENT ON HUMILITY

The Path of the Genie in not linear; it is cyclic. All the stations along this path are inter-related. Consider this: to experience spiritual transformation, you must become aware of your present spiritual condition. Transformation happens when you recognize your spiritual source, desire earnestly to change, and then *surrender* to that spiritual source (or power). *Surrender* is the essence of humility. You cannot undergo transformation without surrender, and you cannot surrender unless you become humble. So humility and self-discovery are closely allied.

Here's an example. Consider Jane to be someone who wants to learn a specific skill. Jane first becomes aware of her present condition—that she is ignorant in that specific skill. She also realizes that someone else has expertise in that skill (comparable to the "spiritual source" mentioned above). Jane surrenders her ego and begins to learn from that skilled practitioner. The result is Jane's transformation from ignorance to competence in that skill.

The greatest obstacle to personal development and becoming the person you ought to be is false pride. If you can let go of your self-absorption and focus on learning and becoming the person you ought to be, you discover the joy of personal growth and spiritual development.

SELF-DISCOVERY LEADS TO MORE HUMILITY

Earlier you read that humility enables you to ask the questions that lead to self-discovery. Interestingly, self-discovery also leads to greater humility – another indication of the cyclic nature of *The Path of the Genie*.

One of the finest men I have had the privilege of knowing was the late Dr. Bill Stump. When I first met him, he was a professor of Chemistry at Virginia Commonwealth University where I attended graduate school. Sharing a common philosophy and faith, we soon became friends.

He once told me about a very dear friend of his who had died of cancer as a young adult. Bill mentioned how, for a long time, he was unable to get past the deep pain he felt at the untimely loss of his friend. No amount of prayer seemed to help.

One day, as Bill was driving, he heard the Beatles on the radio singing the words, "Let it be, let it be, let it be, let it be, someday we'll know the answer, let it be, let it be…" Those words spoke to him. They penetrated his shield of pain and entered his weeping heart. Bill said that was when he was able to let it go … let the pain go, and let his friend go to a place where there is no more pain or crying or sorrow.

He was able to let go because he knew who he was and in whom he believed. Because Bill was able to let go, he was able to get on with living his life, fulfilling his destiny. Self-discovery strengthens one's humility and frees one to let go of the things that he cannot control or understand.

Buddha, the founder of Buddhism said it very directly and simply: "Learn to let go. That is the key to happiness."

UNIQUE GIFTS

Knowing yourself and becoming the person you ought to be invariably leads to asking the third question: "What are my unique gifts?" Here are some questions to ask yourself. What skills or abilities come naturally to me? What activity do I excel in, even if I haven't had much training in it? What puts a glint in my eyes, a song in my heart, and a deep contentment in my soul?

Why is it important to discover and build on your gifts? One lesson that life has taught me is that *you feel fulfilled when you use your unique gifts to achieve significant personal goals and make a positive difference in the world.*

Educator and author Parker J. Palmer explained the above with great insight: "Every human being is born with some sort of gift, an inclination or an instinct that can become a full-blown mastery. We may not see our gift for what it is. Having seen it we may choose not to accept the gift and its consequences for our lives. Or, having claimed our gift, we may not be willing to do the hard work necessary to nurture it. But none of these evasions can alter the fact that the gift is ours. Each of us is a master at something, and part of becoming fully alive is to discover and develop our birthright competence."

What Parker Palmer calls "birthright competence" is what I term "gifts." Your gifts will suggest how you are supposed to spend your time. When you discover your unique gifts and know who you are, you will discover your life's purpose.

> **Each of us is a master at something, and part of becoming fully alive is to discover and develop our birthright competence.**
> **—Parker J. Palmer**

PURPOSE GIVES MEANING

Why is a sense of purpose so important? A sense of purpose gives meaning to your life. When that sense of purpose is closely tied to your self-identity, your transforming self, and your unique gifts, you will find that your life has a special passion—a desire to fulfill your life's purpose.

This is not the kind of fleeting passion that explodes like fireworks in a blaze of glory and then is gone in a puff of smoke. No, it's the kind of passion that sustains a dream long after the sun has set on the day…the kind of passion that overcomes setbacks and obstacles and ploughs on, regardless of disappointments and nay-sayers. It might even lead to changing your career.

Finding your purpose involves discovering who you are, what your unique gifts are, and finding work or a calling that taps your natural gifts; at the same time, it is consistent with your identity and priorities.

PERSONAL TRANSFORMATION

It was not so long ago that I found myself asking questions relating to self-discovery. Due to financial considerations, I chose to do graduate work in chemistry, because as a graduate student I drew a teaching assistant's stipend, which allowed me to survive financially while working toward a doctorate.

After completing my doctorate, I worked as an industrial scientist for about ten years before I fully realized that I was not in the right field for me. While the questions of matter, energy, and the transformation of matter were fascinating to me, and while I had a great deal of theoretical knowledge about them, I realized that I had no natural gifts for practical work in those areas. A Ph.D. in chemistry was not an antidote to the lack of fulfillment that I felt in my work.

At the same time, my active involvement in a Toastmasters Club resulted in my rediscovering my love for public speaking. I tested my skills in speech contests and discovered that I still had a great deal to learn. The desire to overcome the obstacles my Asian accent posed for American audiences and to excel in speech contests led me to hire a coach who was an expert in speech communication and speech pathology.

In addition, I sought advice from former World Champions of Public Speaking and other outstanding speakers, reaping the benefits of their experience and generous guidance. In 1992, I achieved one of my ambitions—to become a finalist at the World Championship of Public Speaking. It was an exciting time for me.

As a result of placing second at the World Championship and being written about in the local newspapers, I received invitations from various organizations to present speeches and seminars. It often happened that following a seminar or keynote speech, someone from the audience would tell me how greatly they had been helped and blessed. The thrill that I felt knowing that I had positively impacted another's life could not be compared to anything else I had experienced in my working life. This was a mind-boggling difference from what I felt when working in a laboratory. Before long, people were asking me how much I charged for my presentations. The joyous thought that came to me was, "Hey, there is money in this!"

I started a part-time business presenting seminars and workshops on weekends and evenings. Four years later, thanks to the loving support of my wife, Sharon, I became a full-time professional speaker, trainer, and speech coach. I've had many lows and many highs, but regardless of the uncertainty my family and I have faced as a result of this career change, I know that I have, at long last, chosen the career path that was meant for me.

Wally "Famous" Amos, who has been described as "the father of the gourmet cookie industry," said it so clearly: "I believe there is something only you can accomplish, an idea with your name on it. It's up to you to grab it and do it or it will never get done." But that is not often easy to discern.

Why do many people fail to give heed to their calling? I believe one reason is that the hard knocks of life, the disappointments, and negative people around them cause many to lose focus on what they could become. Then they settle for the comfortable, humdrum, and less challenging life. But I think that in that case, there will always be a still, small voice whispering to them: "I wonder what you could have accomplished if you had stayed with your dream."

The wildly popular movie, *Sea Biscuit*, was about a great racehorse. Before Sea Biscuit was "discovered," he was considered a second rate, used up, mediocre racehorse. When the extremely gifted horse trainer, Tom Smith, first set his eyes on Sea Biscuit, he saw something in the horse that no one else could see.

In the movie, when talking to others about what he sees in this cast-off racehorse, Tom Smith says, "I just can't help feeling he's forgotten what he was born to do. He just needs to learn to be a horse again." Under the gentle and expert tutelage of the trainer and his jockey, Sea Biscuit eventually discovers the joy of exercising his unique gift of heart and muscle, the sheer joy of excelling in his calling. If a horse can discover his calling, so can you.

SIGNS OF YOUR GIFTS

What you enjoyed doing as a child often reveals your natural gifts. A reporter interviewed a young woman who teaches yoga. The yoga instructor mentioned to the reporter that when she was a child, well before she heard about yoga, she would handle frustration and stress by bending over backwards or standing on her head. Someone told her that she should try yoga. When she was intro-

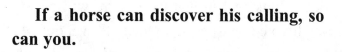

If a horse can discover his calling, so can you.

duced to the world of yoga, her perspective on life itself changed. Now, as an adult, she is living out her calling.

Looking back to my childhood, I see the signs of my "calling." When I was a child, I remember playing stump speaker with another boy. We would climb on a box and give political speeches to each other. I took this so seriously that I wrote out my speeches on a note pad. When I was in high school, I was a member of the debating team. When I was majoring in chemistry in college, I took every oral communications course available as an elective for me because they were "fun" courses that I was good at and enjoyed. Back then, I considered a communications career impractical for me because I didn't think that I had any prospects of finding a well-paying job in the field of communications when I returned to my homeland. Twelve years into my first career as a scientist, I returned full circle to that inner calling.

I can remember my brother Ranjan taking delight as a child in playing for hours with a set of small plastic building blocks to create interesting structures. He has gone on to become an engineer. Kate Smith, the great singer whose rendition of 'God Bless America' made it America's "second national anthem" loved to sing as a child. Instead of taking voice training, she chose the "more practical" field of nursing until the day she decided to pursue her dream of a singing career. What was it that connected with you as a child? Consider that a clue to the special gift you can give the world.

Sometimes the passion for our unique journey hits us late in life. It may come as an awakening. For example, Bill Gore was a research scientist for Du Pont for many years. He believed that the newly synthesized and patented material, poly(tetrafluoroethylene) or "PTFE," now commonly known as "Teflon®," had great potential. However, the Du Pont Company was not interested in the end-uses he envisioned. Determined to sell manufactured goods from PTFE, and much to the shock of many friends and peers, he left Du Pont to start his own company. The "calling" to do this work was stronger than the security of a job and subsequent comfortable retirement from one of the world's best-known chemical companies.

Bill Gore started his manufacturing company in his basement. He had a handful of employees who believed in his vision. In those early days, he sometimes had to ask his employees to wait for their paychecks. Gradually, the business slowly began to get on its feet. One day his son, Robert Gore, made a seminal discovery—how to make expanded PTFE; a material which has unusual and unique properties. This was the beginning of a new industry that led to a multi-million dollar worldwide enterprise. Millions of athletes and outdoorsmen know the material as Gore-Tex®. It all began when a man who was comfortably settled in his career, listened to and acted on the trumpet call of his destiny.

Mary Kay Ash began her company after retiring from a 25-year sales career. She took a great risk. What most people don't know is that Mary Kay Ash's husband, who was to be intimately involved in running her new company, died shortly before they were scheduled to open. Both her attorney and her accountant advised her against starting the company. Her risk was that her venture would collapse; she would lose her life savings and end up penniless. Yet, encouraged by her family and buoyed up by their faith and support, she pressed forward with her plans. The rest, as they say, is history. Today, Mary Kay, Inc. is an international, billion-dollar company that has blessed lives and created incomes for millions of women.

Writing her story in *A Second Helping of Chicken Soup for the Woman's Soul*, Mary Kay Ash says, "…I just decided that retirement did not suit me. And so I developed a strategy and philosophy for beginning my own 'Dream Company.'"

Mary Kay, like Bill Gore, listened to her inner call and lived out her destiny despite a different direction she had taken in years past. In exercising the courage to discover a new dimension of herself, she has helped thousands of women worldwide discover their potential too.

Antonio Stradivari was a 17th century violinmaker whose violin making ability has never been matched. To own a "Stradivarius" is to possess a treasure. The purity of its tones, the velvety smoothness of its notes, and the majestic resonance of a Stradivarius in the hand of a master violinist is more than a thing of beauty.

How did Stradivari create such masterpieces? Hear it from his lips: "When any master holds 'twixt chin and hand a violin of mine, he will be glad that Stradivari lived, made violins and made them of the best...if my hand slipped I should rob God...since he is the fullest good...(But) he could not make Antonio Stradivari's violins without Antonio."

The famous jurist Oliver Wendell Holmes said, "Most of us go to our graves with our music still inside us." Don't keep your music bottled up. Discovering your music is an important step to discovering yourself. What are you called to be and to do?

DREAM DESTROYERS

Why do so many people fail to tap their unique gifts and live the lives that they wish they could? For some, the reason is that they never allow themselves to believe that they have a unique gift to give to the world. There are others who are scared of the responsibility that would be theirs if they acknowledge their gifts and feel an obligation to give them to the world. Perhaps one of the saddest situations is when parents deny the right of their children to follow the paths that their hearts and talents dictate.

HOW PARENTS CAN STEAL A DREAM

In the movie *Dead Poets Society*, Robin Williams stars as an English teacher named Mr. John Keating at a stuffy boys' school. Mr. Keating makes a bunch of boys aware of the beauty and power of poetry and self-expression.

The boys form a "Dead Poets Society." Secretly meeting in a cave, away from the regimented life of their school, they recite poems to one another and revel in the freedom of the spirit they feel when the power of expression unleashes their creative spirits.

One of the boys, whose name is Neil, discovers for the first time what he wants to do with his life. He wants to be an actor. He knows that his father is vehemently against such a course. His father has picked his career path for him— medicine. Neil discovers his talent for acting when, contrary to his father's orders, he stars in a school play. His dad, livid with anger, yanks him out of school, takes him home, and tells him that he will be sent to another school; from there he will go to medical school and eventually become a doctor. "Don't you understand," he shouts at Neil, "You have opportunities that I never had!"

Neil sees the end of his dream. He gives up trying to communicate to a father who will not allow for any dream other than the future that he has plotted for his son. In that dramatic heart-rending scene with his parents, Neil flops on a chair, recalling the crowning glory of his short life, his stirring performance on stage. He says wistfully to himself, "I was good. I was really good." It has to be a statement of the past, not the present or the future, because he sees no possibility of a future for him in the path that his father has decreed. All his mother does is listen sympathetically to his declaration and say, "Go on, get some sleep."

I suspect that this scene or some variation of it is played over and over again in many families around the world. This is especially likely in cultures that are very traditional or in homes where the parents have been through hard times. Such parents often wish for their children the paths that they themselves would have taken if they had had the same opportunities that their children now have.

With good intentions, the parents push their agenda on their child, ignorant to the fact that their child must discover his or her own special gift and calling in order to find fulfillment. In *Dead Poet's Society*, Neil's mother told him to "Get some sleep," but it is such well-meaning parents who are asleep. They are asleep to the reality that their actions may be self-centered. In their blind ambition for their long-deferred dreams to be lived out in the lives of their children, the parents can kill the dreams of the children they love.

During a visit to Sri Lanka, I had the pleasure of speaking at a highly regarded girls' school. Speaking to an audience of several hundred high school girls, I described the elements of self-discovery and challenged them to find their unique gifts and make their special contributions to the world.

Afterwards, several girls approached me and asked me what they should do about the fact that their parents insisted that they follow a course of study that the girls themselves did not want. The parents wanted their girls to become doctors or scientists, not artists or journalists.

The girls knew what they wanted to study and contribute to the world, but the expectations of their parents clashed with their dreams. This was a replay of the movie, *Dead Poets Society*. All I could do was give them advice similar to what Mr. Keating (Robin Williams) gave Neil in that movie: "Talk with your parents. Help them awaken to the fact that your talents and desires are contrary to the direction that they have plotted for you. Take steps to develop your talents and skills and expose your parents to your gifts. Try to bring your parents into your hopes and dreams."

Parents can rightfully point out that their children are not mature enough to make important decisions such as their future career. In such a case, parents can make the effort to find out what their childrens' natural gifts and talents are and steer them toward careers that are congruent with those gifts.

What happens too often is that the father or mother

never discovered their self-identity. Frustrated with their own lives, they force their children to live out the parental dreams. Doing so is stealing from their children, from themselves, and from society. Can you imagine Albert Einstein being forced to become a lawyer, Laurence Olivier being forced to become a physician, or Martin Luther King, Jr. being forced to become an accountant?

A bright spot in the system of education in the United States is that children are given guidance on how to discover a career that's right for them. As I write this, my son Alex is doing a homework assignment for his "Careers" class. In that class he has taken tests to determine his aptitudes. For his homework assignment, he took two personality assessments at two websites, and now he is completing a questionnaire on three occupations that appeal to him. In Alex's first month in ninth grade he took a "Differential Aptitude Test," which was designed to reveal his strengths and aptitudes. This kind of focused attention on the unique strengths of each person bodes well for children discovering the paths that are right for each of them.

TO STEAL A DREAM IS TO
MUTE ANOTHER'S MUSIC

Dream stealing is not confined to parents. Dream stealers are usually people who are close to you and who scoff at your dreams and goals. An old *Reader's Digest* magazine carried a story written by a young woman about her late father. Although her father's occupation was in the field of business, he always wanted to be a writer. Because his wife had repeatedly berated him for "wasting" his time on such an "impractical" ambition, he stopped his efforts at writing...or seemed to have.

After his death, when his daughter was going through his personal effects, she found a box full of clippings of articles he had written and published, as well as letters to editors of out-of-town newspapers. He had kept all this from his wife. You could say that he played his music very quietly because he was afraid that the audience that mattered to him the most, his wife, would mock him. Oh, if we would only listen to the heartbeats of others, and coax them to give to the world their unique music.

Writer Delfina Martinez expresses these thoughts with clarity and elegance: "The inner voice speaks to us all. Some of us listen and hear and give ourselves to being what we were created to be—not the person who society and culture approves of or wants or supports. That is discipline—to be everything that we are potentially able to be by doing the little tedious things which bring us to full potential."

LET YOUR LIGHT SHINE

Sometimes people don't want to discover themselves or their unique gifts because, although they do not feel fulfilled and sense that something is missing, they are comfortable with their station in life. You could say they are in a comfortable rut. As an old saying goes, "A rut is a coffin with the ends knocked off." Their lives are not inspiring to themselves or to others, and there is little to challenge them. They live to survive, not to be victors. In the words of Theodore Roosevelt, "[They] live in the gray twilight that knows neither victory nor defeat." As a result, the world will never know what they could have contributed to life.

Marianne Williamson in her book, *A Return to Love*, expressed this thought exceedingly eloquently. (Nelson Mandela quoted this moving passage in his inaugural address when he became president of South Africa.)

"Our deepest fear is not that we are inadequate. Our deepest fear is that we are powerful beyond measure. It is our light, not our darkness that most frightens us. We ask

> **As you shine, you will discover the joy of illuminating your world.**

ourselves, 'Who am I to be brilliant, gorgeous, talented, fabulous?' Actually, who are you not to be? You are a child of God. Your playing small does not serve the world. There's nothing enlightened about shrinking so that other people won't feel insecure around you. We are all meant to shine, as children do. We were born to make manifest the glory of God that is within us. It's not just in some of us; it's in everyone. And as we let our own light shine, we unconsciously give other people permission to do the same. As we are liberated from our own fear, our presence automatically liberates others."

Discover your light. Let it shine. And if the light isn't

very bright, learn how to make it brighter. As you shine, you will discover the joy of illuminating your world.

When you engage in work that is congruent with your gifts and values, you live a life consistent with your passions. In such a life, there is no such word as "job." It is all play, and you can't imagine not doing what you do. In *The Best of Bits and Pieces*, Dr. W. Gifford-Jones shares: "Never retire. Michelangelo was carving the Rondanini just before he died at 89. Verdi finished his opera Falstaff at 80. At age 80, Spanish artist Goya scrawled on a drawing, "I am still learning."

One of my writer friends, Brian Phillips, once pointed out to me that writers don't need to retire. Of the writers who published in the year 2000, Saul Bellow, Philip Roth, and Joseph Heller were all over 70 years of age. My mother, Anne Abayasekara, who is nearing eighty years of age, has been a journalist for more than 50 years. She continues to practice her craft; it is joy, not work. She knows that she is helping to create a better world.

THE CALL

So far we have considered the vital steps to self-discovery: knowing yourself, becoming the person you are meant to be, and discovering your unique gifts. But life is not always so ordered. Consider people who had a different path to their self-discovery: Buddha, Moses, Saint Paul, and Joan of Arc.

THE CALL CAN BE ILLOGICAL

Prince Siddhartha Gautama lived about 500 years before Christ. He was born into privilege and wealth in a small kingdom now called southern Nepal. He had everything that he could want in terms of material pleasures and comforts. But upon seeing the ravages of old age, disease, and death, he developed a burning desire to discover what causes suffering and how people could escape such suffering. Driven by this "calling," the young prince renounced his inheritance, left his wife and son, and went out into the world in search of the truth. His enlightenment led to the founding of one of the world's great religions, Buddhism. Prince Siddhartha's self-discovery is an example of an inner call that was contrary to all logical expectations. This is what I refer to as "The Call."

Moses was a nomad in the dessert when "The Call" came to him. He was born a Hebrew, but was adopted by an Egyptian princess who brought him up as an Egyptian prince with all the attendant pleasures and privileges. Eventually his spirit was stirred against the injustices to the enslaved Hebrew people. The result: he killed an Egyptian for being cruel to a Hebrew and so had to flee Egypt. Into this scene came the voice of God, calling Moses to lead his people, the Hebrews, out of the land of bondage into a new land of freedom and promise.

Moses did not think that he had any special gift or ability to succeed at what God was calling him to do. He was afraid to go back to Egypt. He knew that he was no public speaker. It seemed highly illogical to him that God would choose him for such a daunting task. So he said, "No." But God kept calling him. God told him to enlist the services of his brother Aaron, who was an eloquent speaker. God, in fact, told him that all He wanted was Moses' availability. He would provide the ability. Moses finally answered this "illogical" call. Moses' obedience to God's call changed the course of history.

THE CALL CAN LEAD TO DRAMATIC TRANSFORMATION

Saul was a passionate Pharisaic Jew who was born many years after Jesus was crucified. He had the equivalent of a Harvard education, having been educated by Gamaliel, one of the renowned scholars and teachers of his time. He came from a wealthy background. He strongly felt the new religious "cult" that proclaimed that Jesus Christ had risen from the dead was a threat to Jewish society. He made it his business to persecute those who followed the teaching of Jesus.

Then one day, on his way to persecute more of these followers of Jesus, he ran smack into "The Call." A blinding bright light shone down on Saul and his companions as they traveled the road to Damascus. He heard a voice saying, "Saul, Saul, why are you persecuting me?" When Saul asked who it was that was speaking, the voice answered, "I am Jesus whom you are persecuting."

That same voice told him to go to Damascus where he

would be told what to do. In Damascus, blind Saul met a man named Ananias who restored his sight. Saul underwent one of the most dramatic transformations recorded in Scripture, when he changed from persecuting Christians into becoming the foremost proponent of the Gospel of Jesus Christ. He blazed a missionary trail throughout Asia Minor and the Roman Empire, setting up churches and writing letters that defined the theology of the church. That was "The Call" that transformed Saul into Saint Paul, the greatest missionary in the history of the Christian Church.

"The Call" is unusual. Most people don't get it. It also is one of the most powerfully transformative events in steering the life of a human being. How else could a 17-year old girl in the fifteenth century lead the French army to vanquish the forces of England and change the course of France's history? That is the story of Joan of Arc, now a patron saint of France and a national heroine. "The Call" reminds us that logic alone, or any formula that we can prescribe, is not the only way to self-discovery. Every instance of "The Call" may not be as dramatic as the above stories, but any of us could experience it.

FROM COMPUTER SALESMAN TO BISHOP

In the mid-1970s, a man who had a great positive influence in my life when I was an undergraduate at the University of Florida was the Pastor of University United Methodist Church, Rev. Robert Fannin. He was simply called "Bob" by the hundreds of university students to whom he ministered. Bob had been a computer salesman who was doing very well in his chosen profession when "The Call" to go into the ministry came to him. It was a call that he could not shake. The result was a change in careers, and a life that has blessed thousands of others. Just a few years ago (and many years after graduating from the University of Florida), I had the pleasure of meeting, once again, this great man who had been such an inspiration to me. This former computer salesman who had answered "The Call" was now a Bishop.

"The Call" reminds us that the Creator looks for availability and obedience more than for ability. But I also believe that the Master Designer of the universe gives us abilities to excel in the work that He has chosen for us.

Know yourself and your values. Discover and use your unique gifts. Live life purposefully. Let your work reflect your gifts. And if you get "The Call," say "Yes." Then you, too, like Aladdin and like so many other fulfilled souls, will be well on your way to achieving your heart's desire.

Now you have seen the power of the wish for humility and the wish for self-discovery. You have traveled part of the way along *The Path of the Genie*. What remains is the point of greatest growth. Once again look to your guide, Aladdin.

FIVE ACTION STEPS
FOR SELF-DISCOVERY

1. **Know God.** Realize that you are a spiritual being having a human experience. Seek to know your creator. You will then come to understand your eternal significance. Most of our struggles have a spiritual root cause. Associate with people who are spiritually mature. Actively seek answers to your spiritual questions.

2. **Understand what gives you bliss.** Ask yourself what gives you a deep sense of fulfillment. If you ever felt deeply fulfilled, ask yourself what were you doing at that time; what were the circumstances? If you can be deeply fulfilled once, you can be deeply fulfilled again, and again, and again...

3. **Discover your gifts.** What do you do extremely well with ease? You may not have much training or education in it, but you do it unusually well. Think back to your childhood also, and recall what you liked to do as a child. You will find clues in your past. Joining a Toastmasters Club can be a catalyst for discovering your gifts. Toastmasters International is the leading volunteer organization in the world for men and women to learn the arts of communication and leadership. In learning to express your heart's yearnings, you will get in touch with the

music of your soul. To find a Toastmasters Club near you, visit www.Toastmasters.org

4. **Work on becoming the person you ought to be.** This is closely tied to knowing who you are spiritually. If you wish your values were different from what they are now, then start living as if you embraced the values that you prefer. Build relationships with people who have lifestyles that you want to emulate. Gradually you will become the person you ought to be.

5. **Build your life around your true identity, your calling, and your gifts.** If your life is not centered around your identity, calling, and gifts, it's important that you get started on that path. Start in a small way. Test yourself in your new venture. You may want to start a new hobby or even a part-time business or move in an entirely new direction from your past. The best way to begin is to just focus on heading in the right direction for you while staying true to your best self. Your heart will tell you if you are doing what you are supposed to be doing.

PART IV

THE THIRD WISH

"…For it is in giving, that we receive,
It is in pardoning, that we are pardoned,
It is in dying, that we are
born again into eternal life."
– St. Francis of Assisi

THE PARADOX OF TRANSFORMATION

What was Aladdin's third wish? You may recall that Aladdin could only make three wishes. He had promised the Genie that he would use his third wish to grant the Genie the one thing that the Genie wanted most—freedom from imprisonment in the lamp. But Aladdin's heart's desire was to become a true prince so that he could fulfill the requirements of the law to win the hand of Princess Jasmine. Yet, he knew that he had promised the Genie that he would use his third wish to gain freedom for the Genie. So Aladdin had to make a tough decision – "Do I live up to my promise and grant the Genie his heart's desire, or do I ignore my promise and just go for *my* heart's desire?"

Aladdin chose to live up to his promise. He denied his own gratification and used his third wish to gain freedom for the Genie. What Aladdin did not know when he made that wish was that he set into motion universal powers that resulted in him gaining his heart's desire – the hand of Princess Jasmine. Aladdin discovered the third wish of The Path of the Genie— *The Wish for Self-Offering.*

This third wish is the culmination of personal development. When you get to this point, your focus is not on receiving, though you are humble and open for growth opportunities. Your focus is not on discovering who you are, because you already know who you are, although you are open to learning more about yourself and your potential.

Your focus in living this third wish can be summarized in three questions:

"How can I give of myself?"

"To whom can I give of myself?"

"What blessing can I give to my world?"

MANKIND IS YOUR BUSINESS

Ebenezer Scrooge is a familiar literary figure who is the antithesis of self-offering as introduced to us in Charles Dickens' *A Christmas Carol*. In the story, the ghost of Scrooge's deceased business partner, Jacob Marley, appears to him in a dream. The ghost of Marley tries to warn Scrooge that he must change, and gives voice to the realization of what is truly important: "Mankind was my business. The common welfare was my business: charity, mercy, forbearance, and benevolence, were all my business. The dealings of my trade were but a drop of water in the comprehensive ocean of my business!"

When Aladdin sacrificed his own desire in order to gain freedom for the Genie, he demonstrated that his journey of discovery had led him to the third wish, the wish for self-offering. Without knowing, Aladdin was practicing what St. Francis of Assisi had prayed for: "It is in giving that we receive; it is in pardoning that we are pardoned; it is in dying that we are born again into eternal life." We could restate that last phrase by saying, "It is in letting go of selfishness that you truly learn to live."

This is a paradox, but it is true. The wish for self-offering is the culmination of self-development. Your focus is not on yourself; your focus is on the welfare of others.

Fortunately, there are many people around us who demonstrate the power of this wish. In his book, *Soul Stories*, best-selling author Gary Zukhov tells of a time that Oprah Winfrey telephoned him. Oprah had told him, "I could retire and count the shoes in my closet, but I want to give something to the world. I want to create television that helps people change their lives." Oprah had entered the sacred station of the third wish of *The Path of the Genie*. Her television shows are a testament to that.

HEROES AMONGST US

You don't have to be a celebrity or a famous person to live this third wish. This third wish is lived out every day in the lives of ordinary people. Some years ago, at a lecture in King of Prussia, Pennsylvania, I heard writer and speaker, Dr. Wayne Dyer, describe a mother who had turned a tragedy into an opportunity to give sacrificially. One of her daughters was severely injured in an accident and was rendered comatose. Since then, that mother has nursed the daughter and stayed by her side almost constantly over many years, keeping her alive, and creating a vortex of hope when life itself appeared to be spinning away from her daughter.

Everyday heroes are everywhere. They are the ones that keep hope alive for many others who have not even begun their journey along *The Path of the Genie*. They do not see themselves as heroes. They are simply continuing on their path. Mothers, fathers, brothers, sisters—every day, little as well as big acts of self-offering are being performed in homes, hospitals, businesses, churches, temples, and synagogues; in restaurants, clubs, civic organizations, and clinics; on roadways, bazaars, and in corners of society that we never hear about. Self-offering is the light that brightens a world that too often is threatened by the forces of darkness.

HEALING AMIDST HURTING

This third wish holds immense power. How powerful is it? Let me share a true story of how those who practice it can bring healing to a hurting world. In Sri Lanka, the Chinniah family was of Tamil ethnic origin, and they were Christian in their chosen faith. The family included a mother, a father, three sisters, and a brother. The father was a physician who had worked in Tissamaharama, a village in the deep south of the island that is dominantly Sinhala in ethnicity and Buddhist in religious tradition. The villagers liked the Tamil doctor who lived and worked in their midst and their affection was extended to his family.

The Chinniah's bought property there and always maintained good relations with the villagers. Later, after their mother and father passed away, the siblings moved to the big city—Colombo—but retained their property and rice paddy fields in Tissamaharama, and kept in touch with the villagers.

In July of 1983, reacting to the killing of Sinhalese soldiers by Tamil separatists, the city of Colombo was wracked with ethnic riots. Mobs of the majority Sinhalese attacked Tamil people, killing and injuring them, and even burning their homes. In a day or so word reached Tissamaharama about the riots in Colombo. Some villagers, concerned about the Chinniah family, took the long trip to Colombo by bus and train. They went to the Chinniahs' house only to find that it had been reduced to a heap of rubble.

Fearing the worst, they inquired from neighbors what had happened to the family. They found out that the Chinniahs were now in a government-run camp for refugees that had been set up at Royal College, my former high school. The villagers went to the refugee camp, met with and comforted the Chinniahs. When the villagers returned to Tissamaharama, they discussed the Chinniah's plight and made the decision to rebuild the Chinniahs' house.

The villagers located and arranged for timber, a truck to transport materials, plumbers, masons, electricians, and all the assorted supplies and expertise needed to rebuild the house. A group of young men came to clear the rubble and provide the manual labor. While the rebuilding campaign was going on, these men built a temporary shelter near the house and brought the Chinniah family out of the refugee camp. A sister of one of the village men even volunteered to cook for the family. The house was rebuilt in a surprisingly short time and the Chinniah family returned to their home.

The crowning moment of these acts of healing and restoration came when a Buddhist priest from the village traveled all the way to Colombo to visit the Chinniahs to apologize for the atrocities that his people had committed against them. These villagers did not see themselves as Sinhala Buddhists and the Chinniahs as Tamil Christians, but simply as fellow human beings like themselves, who had suffered undeservedly.

These humble people lived the third wish of the path of the Genie—the wish for self-offering. They answered those three important questions: "How can I give of myself? To whom can I give of myself? What blessing can I give to my world?"

BEYOND SUCCESS TO SIGNIFICANCE

Some years ago *The Patriot-News* of Harrisburg, Pennsylvania, published a story about a middle-aged couple, Earl and Chris Mummert, who practiced this art of self-offering. In the words of Earl Mummert, "We wanted to use our financial success as an enabling tool to do something very meaningful with our lives." The Mummerts, who had retired early, traveled to Slovakia to help alleviate the great need for English teachers. They spent nine months there. Chris taught English as a second language in a Lutheran church-sponsored high school, while Earl did consulting work for the Bishop of the Lutheran Synod there and also served as "househusband." Nine months of absence could have really hurt their business influence, but that did not have the highest priority item in their lives. As Earl indicated, they wanted to turn their "success into significance."

Before they left Slovakia, Chris Mummerts' students

presented her with a journal that they had written. One student wrote: "You have given us so much more than just the rules of English, but the lessons of life." That was success and significance. The Mummerts had made a positive difference by the choices they made.

The motivation for self-offering is not personal glory. The motivation to give arises when an individual has attained a level of personal growth that seeks satisfaction in helping others grow. Such a person knows that his life has a purpose that is tied to the well being of others. He or she is an artist, a creator and sustainer of beauty in others. As Charlie "Tremendous" Jones says, "Don't simply help others. Help others learn how to help others."

HOW MUCH IS YOUR
SELF-OFFERING WORTH?

There is a story of a nun in an orphanage that reminds me of self-offering and its motivation. A man was visiting the orphanage at the same time that the children were sitting down for breakfast. The visitor noticed a young nun who was trying to help a little boy who appeared to be spastic. With an involuntary jerk, the little boy sent his breakfast plate, juice, and milk flying down to spatter on the floor. The nun immediately consoled the boy, turned him over to another attendant, and got down on her hands and knees to clean the mess on the floor.

The man, watching, blurted out, "I don't know how you do this work. I wouldn't do it for a million dollars!" The young nun looked him straight in the eyes and said, "I wouldn't do it for a million dollars either."

To the person who practices self-offering, the reward is in the good that it does for others. Sometimes, from a worldly point of view, the practice of self-offering may appear to be contrary to common sense. Instead of saying, "Look out for number one," the spirit of self-offering says, "Look out for others." You can do that because you are whole; because you know who you are and that you are in the care of a power greater than yourself. This sense of

The motivation for self-offering is not personal glory. The motivation to give arises when an individual has attained a level of personal growth that seeks satisfaction in helping others grow.

assurance allows you to forget yourself and focus on helping others.

The wish for self-offering makes sense when you look at the world with a new perspective. That is possible when you travel through the stations of humility and self-discovery. That is when the prayer of St. Francis of Assisi makes sense.

KNOCK, KNOCK – REJECTION, READING, RENEWAL

How do you go from being self-focused to becoming "other-focused?" Let me share with you a life experience that was instrumental in that transition for me.

As a college junior, I came upon a job opportunity that became one of the great learning experiences of my life. The Southwestern Company engaged me (along with several thousand college students from around the country) as an independent contractor to sell books door-to-door during the summer. What would prompt sane young people to even consider taking such a job? In my case it was financial need and the potential for earning more money in one summer than could be earned in a minimum wage job over an entire year. The fact that I would work in States and towns far removed from where I lived also added to the attraction.

A week of sales training at the company headquarters in Franklin, Tennessee, made me feel like I could sell sunshine to Hawaiians. I was assigned to a small team of students and deployed to sell books in several small towns. I had no idea that there was a magical learning experience waiting for me when I went up to a stranger's house, knocked on the door, and when it was opened, flashed my brilliant smile and said: "Hi Mrs. Jones, my name is Dilip. I'm with the Southwestern Company. I'm talking with folks who have school-age children. May I come in?"

The toughest thing that a door-to-door salesperson has

93

to get used to is the rejection. What I didn't realize at first was that this rejection was going to severely test my belief in myself and in the value of what I was doing. Unlike the other students on my team, I was fortunate in that I had no home to go to if I quit my job. I could not retreat into a safe haven. The only road open was the path in front of me. So, after both my team members quit and went home, I plugged on. After going through a valley of despair (and a few tears of exasperation), almost miraculously I hit a patch of good luck and made a bunch of sales. My confi-

I thought that I had signed up for a summer job. What I received was a priceless education in the value of hard work, persistence, and human relations.

dence picked up and my sales continued to increase. Soon I learned to laugh at the occasional sign near a doorway that read, "We shoot every third peddler. The second one just left." I even learned to keep my cool when a man pointed a shotgun at me and told me that I had ten seconds to get off his property. But the acceptance and kindness that I experienced far outweighed any negatives.

I ended that summer with a stronger sense of self and knowledge and understanding about people. I thought that I had signed up for a summer job. What I received was a priceless education in the value of hard work, persistence, and human relations. Without knowing it, I was advancing along the *Path of the Genie.*

It was the next summer that I experienced my greatest growth in this door-to-door adventure. My sales team consisted of three college buddies I recruited to join me in this "summer job." One of them was Tommy Thompson who, like me, realized that there was a good reason that the Southwestern Company gave us great reading material like the books *Life is Tremendous* by Charlie "Tremendous" Jones, *The Magic of Thinking Big* by David Schwartz, and *The Greatest Salesman in the World* by Og Mandino. This last book played a big role in sustaining us that summer. Whenever Tommy and I could coordinate our schedules, we met for breakfast at a nearby McDonalds restaurant and read aloud one of the "Scrolls" of *The Greatest Salesman in the World*.

The message in each of the ten scrolls in *The Greatest Salesman in the World* is inspiring, but I think our favorite was "The Scroll Marked II." It started in this manner: "I will greet this day with love in my heart. For this is the greatest secret of success in all ventures. Muscle can split a shield and even destroy life but only the unseen power of love can open the hearts of men and until I master this art I will remain no more than a peddler in the market place. I will make love my greatest weapon and none on whom I call can defend against its force. My reasoning they may counter; my speech they may distrust; my apparel they may disapprove; my face they may reject; and even my bargains may cause them suspicion; yet my love will melt all hearts liken to the sun whose rays soften the coldest clay. I will greet this day with love in my heart." After reading that scroll, Tommy and I would go on our separate routes, our spirits renewed and fired up to knock on our first doors by 8:00 a.m. with a smile on the face and love in the heart.

Tommy and I were discovering how one becomes "other-centered." When I had love in my heart, instead of trying to make a quick sale, I focused on my prospective customers' needs and how best my books could help them. Something interesting happened with this approach. I had more fun, had more pride in the value I was providing to my customers, and sold more books! If Aladdin had met me then, he might have grinned and said, "Welcome to the station of self-offering."

The wish for self-offering makes sense when you look at the world with a new perspective. That is possible when you travel through the stations of humility and self-discovery. That is when the prayer of St. Francis of Assisi makes sense.

YOU CHOOSE—FRAGRANCE OR SMELL?

Wherever you are on your path, the truth is that you will influence people around you. I recall a humorous story of a woman going to a perfume counter to return a small bottle of perfume. Puzzled, the salesclerk asked the woman what the problem was, because it was one of their most expensive perfumes. The woman gave a baleful look at her boyfriend and said, "I don't like the man it attracted!"

Everyone influences others, for good or bad. You can be a fragrance that attracts or a smell that repels. When you embrace the wish for self-offering, you become a fragrance that attracts the best in others. This means that you deliberately offer yourself and your gifts to make a positive difference in the lives of others.

If you don't think you can make a difference, keep in mind former Congressman Sam Ewing's observation, "If you think that one person can't make a difference in today's world, just light up a cigar in a crowded restaurant!"

GROWING INTO GIVING

Shortly before famous bodybuilder and film star Arnold Schwarzenneger entered the race for Governor of California, the writer Dotson Rader interviewed him. Schwarzenegger's words, as reported by Rader in *Parade* magazine, reveal the evolution of a person toward selflessness. "In the beginning, I was selfish," Schwarzenegger had told him. "It was all about, 'How do I build Arnold? How can I win the most Mr. Universe and Mr. Olympia titles? How can I get into the movies and get into business?' I was thinking about myself."

As he achieved mega success and matured, Schwarzenegger changed his focus. He founded the Inner City Games Foundation, which provides educational, sports, arts, and technology programs year-round for 250,000 kids in 15 cities. In 2002, he authored and campaigned for Proposition 49, a ballot initiative mandating state grants to every California elementary and middle school for after-school programs. Schwarzenegger told Rader, "I think your life is judged not by how much you have taken but by how much you give back."

Self-offering requires a mindset that is different from one that is only focused on success or achievement for yourself. Self-offering requires the heart of a servant. The late Robert Greenleaf introduced the term 'servant leadership' to the lexicon of modern leadership studies. He introduced the paradigm of leadership, not as people who receive special privileges, but as those who sacrificially serve their followers. This is not a new concept. Many of the great spiritual masters voiced this concept.

I think your life is judged not by how much you have taken but by how much you give back.

Arnold Schwarzenegger

The Buddha taught his followers to be willing to sacrifice their lives to preserve the lives of others, even animals. When two of his disciples were jousting to position themselves to sit by his side when he came into his kingdom, Jesus said, "He that would be the greatest must be the servant of all." The person whose objective is self-glory, focuses only on his own success, but the person whose objective is to serve focuses on the success of those he serves. Your greatest success is the success of those you influence.

THE LEGACY OF JIM MILLER

It is very common for the average person to wonder what he or she can offer to the world. I could think, "If I were rich or powerful or had political connections, I could do something. But I'm just an unknown person who has no wealth, fame or influence. What good can *I* do?" Consider this story about a person who chose to do what he could. It was in an e-mail forwarded to me by Todd Milano, President of Central Pennsylvania College. The author is unknown.

"During the waning years of the depression in a small Idaho community, I used to stop by Mr. Miller's roadside stand for farm fresh produce as the season made it available. Food and money were extremely scarce, and bartering was used extensively."

"One day Mr. Miller was bagging some early potatoes for me. I noticed a small boy, delicate of bone and feature, ragged, but clean, hungrily appraising a basket of freshly picked green peas."

"I paid for my potatoes, but also was drawn to the display of fresh green peas. I am a pushover for creamed peas and new potatoes. Pondering the peas, I couldn't help overhearing the conversation between Mr. Miller and the ragged boy next to me."

"Hello Barry, how are you today?"

"H'lo, Mr. Miller. Fine, thank ya. Jus' admirin' them peas…sure look good."

"They are good, Barry. How's your ma?"

"Fine. Gittin' stronger alla time."

"Good. Anything I can help you with?"

"No, sir. Jus' admirin' them peas."

"Would you like to take some home?"

"No, sir. Got nothin' to pay for 'em with."

"Well, what have you to trade me for some of those peas?"

"All I got's my prize marble here."

"Is that right? Let me see it."

"Here 'tis. She's a dandy."

"I can see that. Hmmm, only thing is this one is blue and I sort of go for red. Do you have a red one like this at home?"

"Not zackley...but almost."

"Tell you what. Take this sack of peas home with you and next trip this way let me look at that red marble."

"Sure will. Thanks Mr. Miller."

"Mrs. Miller who had been standing nearby, came over to help me. With a smile she said, "There's two other boys like him in our community; all three are in very poor circumstances. Jim just loves to bargain with them for peas, tomatoes, or whatever. When they come back with their red marbles, and they always do, he decides he doesn't like red after all, and he sends them home with a bag of produce for a green marble or an orange one, perhaps."

"I left the stand smiling to myself, impressed with this man, the boys, and their bartering."

"Several years went by, each more rapid than the previous one. Just recently I had occasion to visit some old friends in that Idaho community and while there, learned that Mr. Miller had died. They were having his viewing that evening and knowing my friends wanted to go, I agreed to accompany them."

"Upon arrival at the mortuary we fell into line to meet the relatives of the deceased and to offer whatever words of comfort we could. Ahead of us in line were three young men. One was in an army uniform and the other two wore nice haircuts, dark suits, and white shirts…all very professional looking."

"They approached Mrs. Miller, standing composed and smiling by her husband's casket. Each of the young men hugged her, kissed her on the cheek, spoke briefly with her and moved on to the casket. Her misty light blue eyes followed them as, one-by-one, each young man stopped briefly and placed his own warm hand over the cold, pale hand in the casket. Each left the mortuary awkwardly, wiping his eyes."

"Our turn came to meet Mrs. Miller. I told her who I was and mentioned the story she had told me about the marbles. With her eyes glistening, she took my hand and led me to the casket."

"Those three young men who just left were the boys I told you about. They just told me how they appreciated the things Jim "traded" them. Now, at last, when Jim can't change his mind about color or size…they came to pay their debt."

"We've never had a great deal of the wealth of this world," she confided, "but right now, Jim would consider himself the richest man in Idaho."

"With loving gentleness she lifted the lifeless fingers of her deceased husband. Resting underneath were three exquisitely shined red marbles."

So if you ever feel like excusing yourself from positively affecting another's life because you don't have wealth or fame, remember the legacy of Jim Miller. Each one of us is a center of influence, whether we accept it or not. You and I can choose to be a fragrance that attracts or a smell that repels. It's all in how we practice the wish for self-offering.

GENIES IN MY LIFE

I am truly blessed. People have blessed me with their sacrificial acts of self-offering far beyond what I ever could have imagined. When I was yearning to attend college in the USA (without sufficient funds to do so), it was the spirit of self-offering that prompted the Nanayakkaras, my Aunt Amy and Uncle Albert in Lake Worth, Florida, to invite me to stay with them, although they were experiencing financial challenges themselves as recent immigrants with a business of their own.

It was the spirit of self-offering that prompted other families like the Joneses, the Knapps, and the Edwards to "adopt" me and make me feel like I was a part of their families. It was the practice of self-offering that led the youth group at Lakeside United Methodist Church to do service jobs one summer to secretly raise money to buy for me, a cash-strapped college student in the USA, a round trip airplane ticket to visit my family half-way around the world.

It was an act of self-offering when the Board of the University United Methodist Church in Gainesville, Florida, offered me an "Upper Room" scholarship that provided me with a room at no charge in exchange for service as a youth leader and for doing light janitorial work. It was the spirit of self-offering on someone's part that led them to anonymously place a pair of new sneakers in my church mailbox when I couldn't afford to buy a new pair. It was an act of self-offering when Jim and Terri Adkins spent their Christmas bonus money to buy me—a homesick, foreign graduate student—a round-trip bus ticket in December of 1982 so that I could spend a wonderful Christmas with their family.

HOW KELLY SHARED
HER FRAGRANCE WITH ME

I personally know how one life can affect another. When I say that, I can see the face of Kelly Weber. Kelly and I first met at a Toastmasters Area Speech Contest. Having heard my competition speech, Kelly introduced herself to me, congratulated me, and then, in her very direct style said, "Dilip, I think you can go all the way." "What do you mean?" was my response. Kelly explained to me that she thought that I had the talent to become a finalist at Toastmasters World Championship of Public Speaking, the highest level of speech competition in the world's premier volunteer organization devoted to helping people develop their communication and leadership skills.

Although I had no shortage of confidence, even to me that seemed a bit of a stretch. However, since I was a fairly new Toastmaster and Kelly was an advanced Toastmaster, her words had an impact on me. She planted the seed of the thought in me that perhaps I could make it to the world championship stage some day.

The next year, I went to my first Toastmasters International Convention, mainly to witness the World Championship of Public Speaking that Kelly had mentioned. There, in a hall packed with more than 1500 people, I listened spellbound to nine of the finest speakers in the world compete for the title, World Champion of Public Speaking. I was in awe of those speakers because I realized that I had a long way to go before I would be able to compete with them, but the speaker's spark in me that Kelly had fanned became brighter.

On the way out of the crowded hall, I accidentally bumped into someone. As we simultaneously said, "Excuse me," we recognized each other. It was Kelly! What were the odds of us bumping into to each other? About 1500 to1. It wasn't a coincidence.

Kelly's eyes opened wide when she saw me. She pulled me to the side. Then she proceeded to tell me what I should do and should not do *when* I became a finalist at the World Championship. Kelly Weber's absolute faith in my destiny to be on that stage was like an elixir to my soul. The speaker's fire in me grew brighter.

A job change took me to another state, and I lost touch with Kelly. However, I remained very active in Toastmasters. Four years later, after many ups and downs in speech contests, I was a finalist at the World Championship of Public Speaking. It had been a long journey, but now I knew that it was all worth it. It was especially exciting when I heard that Kelly was in the audience.

The moment of truth came in 1992 on a Saturday morning on stage in Las Vegas in front of 2300 people. I could hardly believe that I was on stage with eight of the best speakers in the Toastmasters world. I gave what I thought was the best speech I had ever given. It felt glorious.

After the competition, there were interviews and announcements. Then, the winners were announced. No, I didn't win. I came in second. But, as competitive as I am, I was surprised that I wasn't upset that I didn't come in number one. Why? Well, I knew that I had achieved a new level of connecting with an audience, and that gave me a deep sense of fulfillment. With Sharon by my side, and my brother Ranjan and his wife Niranjala visiting from Australia, I was on one of the greatest natural highs that I have ever experienced.

When the event was over, my immediate thought was to find Kelly. My wife and I found her husband Dick, and he told us that Kelly was very ill and had been unable to attend the contest. Knowing how much I wanted to see her, he said that we could visit her for a few minutes.

When Sharon and I saw Kelly, we were shocked at the

change in her appearance. She was suffering from acute diabetes. The doctors had done all they could for her. She had aged a great deal, and the glint in her eyes had disappeared. I bent down and held her hand and told her that I had been on that stage that she had told me about when we first met. For a moment, it seemed to me that her old fire came back into her eyes. In a weak, but very sincere voice, she told me that if she had known that I was one of the finalists, she would have been there in the audience. I knew that she would have. We chatted for a few minutes, but it was obvious that she was tiring fast. I told Kelly how much I appreciated her encouragement and belief in me. With an embrace and kiss, we reluctantly bid her and Dick goodbye.

The next evening, after Sharon and I had returned home, we received a phone call from the President of Toastmasters International. Dick Weber had asked him to call us to let us know that Kelly had passed away that morning. She had gone on to glory 24 hours after my appearance at the World Championship of Public Speaking. In my heart, I figuratively fell to my knees and gave thanks for the fragrance of Kelly Weber's life. The memory of her encouragement and fervent belief in me will forever warm my bones.

You are a center of influence. Like Kelly, you can choose to exercise your influence to bless others, or you can choose to ignore the opportunities to spread your fragrance. I strongly believe that due to your life's peculiarities and circumstances you are in a position to specifically bless someone. If you withhold that blessing, that person will never receive that special blessing that only you can give.

DON'T WAIT FOR THE SIGNIFICANT

Perhaps one reason that people sometimes don't exercise this wish for self-offering is because they are waiting until they can do something really "significant." In such instances, they fail to realize that any act of self-offering, however small, can make a big difference in someone else's life.

One evening, after a church supper, I noticed that one

> **I strongly believe that due to your life's peculiarities and circumstances you are in a position to specifically bless someone.**

of the members of the church staff, whom I had always admired for her untiring and dedicated work with children, looked strained and tired. It was a simple act of encouragement for me to touch her on the shoulder and tell her how much I appreciated her work. The transformation on her face was as if a light bulb had been turned on. A couple of days later I received a card from her telling me that my words of encouragement and appreciation had made a big difference for her that day because she had been feeling down.

You can never predict how one small act of self-offering can make a big difference in someone else's life. Ask the leper whom Mother Teresa hugged. Ask a child whose fears a loving mother or father has assuaged. Ask yourself when you recall the times when someone's self-offering elevated your life. Remind yourself of the quiet satisfaction you felt when you made a positive difference for someone else.

Leo Tolstoy summed up this wish for self-offering very succinctly when he wrote, "Joy can be real only if people look upon their life as a service, and have a definite object in life outside themselves and their personal happiness."

FIVE ACTION STEPS FOR SELF-OFFERING

1. **Get this priceless perspective.** Understand that everything you have is a gift from God. You can call "God" the Universe or the Great Spirit or whatever you choose. Every breath you take, your family, your job, and every possession you have is a gift. You can't take that with you when you die. What matters is what you do with your gifts while you are alive. What really matters is the positive difference you make in the lives of others. Until you claim this perspective, you will never fully realize the joy and freedom of self-offering.

2. **Build self-offering into your lifestyle.** Every action begins with a thought. When you guide your thoughts, you will guide your actions. When you guide your actions, you will create purposeful

habits. When you create purposeful habits, you will build service-oriented character. When you build such character, you will create a lifestyle of enduring value…a lifestyle marked by self-offering.

3. **Learn from Others.** There are people you know whose lives demonstrate the caring, compassionate, and life-building power of self-offering. Observe them, read about them, think about them, and learn from them.

4. **Don't forget little actions.** You don't have to go on a mission to a faraway country to make a positive difference in someone's life. There are many little things that you can do that could make a big difference for someone. Listening to a troubled teenager, writing a note of condolence to a grieving friend, bringing flowers home for your loved one for no reason other than to tell her that you love her, giving a word of encouragement to someone who is discouraged; these are all examples of powerful little actions.

5. **Leave a legacy that carries on your good work.** A legacy is what stays behind after you've passed from this life. You could say your legacy marks the spot of your life on the timeline of human history. Your legacy could be human lives changed for the better. It could be a family that has been blessed by your life. It could be an organization or institution

that creates value for people. It could be a thing of beauty that brings joy and inspiration to others. Live your life in such a way that your good works will outlive you.

PART V

THE CIRCLE OF FULFILLMENT

"In the circle of life

It's the wheel of fortune

It's the leap of faith

It's the band of hope

Till we find our place

On the path unwinding

In the circle of life, the circle of life."

– Elton John

THE CIRCLE OF FULFILLMENT

The Path of the Genie shows the way for you to gain your heart's desire. The three wishes create the Circle of Fulfillment, as shown below.

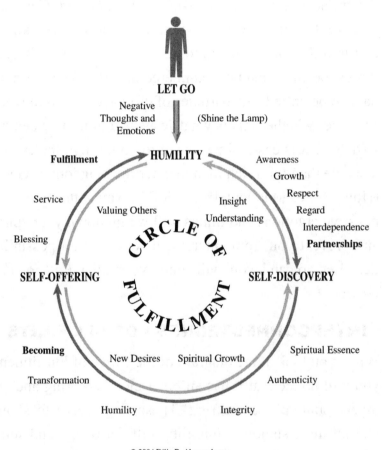

© 2004 Dilip R. Abayasekara

The Circle of Fulfillment

ENTERING THE CIRCLE OF FULFILLMENT

When you let go of pride, envy, jealousy and other blights of the spirit, you allow yourself to hear the still, small voice of guidance within you. This "letting go" is the entrance to the circle of fulfillment. If there were a sign at the entrance, it would say: *No baggage allowed. Come as you are.* If you've ever tried to thread a needle, you know that in order for the thread to go through the needle's eye, it must be clean and unencumbered of dirt or knots. Knots have to be untied, and particles of dirt have to be removed. I wonder whether this is what Jesus had in mind when he said, " ... it is easier for a camel to go through the eye of a needle than for a rich man to enter the kingdom of God" (Holy Bible, Matthew 19:24, KJV). Your attachment to negative emotions and things will weigh down your spirit and prevent you from entering the circle of all possibilities. Let go, and you will enter your own *Path of the Genie*.

INTERCONNECTEDNESS OF ALL PARTS

When you look at the diagram of the Circle of Fulfillment you will notice that it has an outer clockwise ring and an inner counterclockwise ring. These rings serve to show that all three stations—humility, self-discovery, and self-offering—are interconnected. When you are humble, you are able to receive the gifts given to you by others who practice self-offering. Receiving those gifts will help you discover more about yourself. As you experience self-discovery, you discover your gifts and achieve at high levels.

High achievement leads to greater self-discovery. Then you start to look outside of yourself at the needs of others. As your awareness grows, you practice self-offering. Then someone else must practice humility to accept your gifts. Thus it goes on and on. This is the circle of fulfillment.

LESSONS OF NATURE, LESSONS OF LIFE

This circle of receiving, growing, and giving can be seen in our interactions with plants. The seed receives water and nutrients from the earth. It then grows ("discovering" itself). The seedling absorbs carbon dioxide and gives out oxygen. We humans breathe in ("receive") the oxygen, necessary for us to live. We tend to saplings, nurture, and water them ("offering"). They grow into trees and provide beauty and shade for us.

If I do not know myself, I will not be able to authentically give myself away.

Consider, too, the cycle of human growth. The child receives the love and protection of his parents. He grows and discovers himself. He becomes able to give to those who need. As his parents age, they have the humility to ask for help. The child, now grown, is able to give of himself to his parents.

Consider this cycle in professional life. A young woman receives guidance from a senior employee at work and learns and grows into a capable professional. She "discovers" who she is and uncovers her unique strengths. She then is able to mentor those who practice the spirit of humility and ask for help and guidance. The circle of fulfillment is the rhythm of life as it was meant to be lived.

YOUR HEART'S DESIRE

Author and philosopher Wayne Dyer says, "If you don't learn from your mistakes, you are doomed to repeat them over and over again." If you don't follow *The Path of the Genie*, then you are doomed to run in place or fall behind. If you choose to follow the path, then you will grow, become the person you were meant to be, and be a positive contributor to the cycle of life. Then you will discover that you have attained your heart's desire. You have entered that wonderful place called "fulfillment."

ONE STEP AT A TIME

Can you skip the first wish or the second wish and only live the third wish? I don't think so. My life experience teaches me that I must go through the process of self-discovery more deeply in order to give a greater blessing to my world. If I do not know myself, I will not be able to authentically give myself away.

My greatest humiliations have happened at the point of my greatest pride. My greatest growth has happened as a result of my being ready for that growth and being open to learn from those who had superior knowledge and wisdom. I don't think that you can simply leapfrog any of the stations in the circle of fulfillment.

NEW EYES ... NEW HORIZONS

A surprising thing has happened as I have trod *The Path of the Genie*. I have changed. My old vision has given way to a new and more exciting understanding of life. In the past I was focused on achieving more and more for myself. Now I'm more interested in living out my potential for bringing blessings into the lives of others.

In the past I was more interested in proving how good I was as a speaker. Now I'm more interested in giving value to my listeners. In the past I was more interested in appearing to be a great husband and father. Now I am more aware of how much I love my wife and children and how much I owe to them. As my vision changed, so did the goals I set for myself.

THE MOTIVATION FOR ACHIEVEMENT

The focus on helping others does not mean that those who follow *The Path of the Genie* are not high achievers. Usually they are. It was in achieving ambitious goals that they made significant self-discoveries. When they exercised the wish for self-offering, it signaled that their priorities had changed from self to others.

Ego-driven people achieve great things with their own glory in mind. Those who tread *The Path of the Genie* also achieve great things. But their motivation for achievement goes beyond ego to being a blessing for others. Think of someone you know who is on this path. Their life is the proof of *The Path of the Genie*.

SIGNS OF AWAKENING

In the past few years there have been an increasing number of reports about families uprooting themselves from rich, corporate lifestyles and resettling themselves in the quiet countryside to live simpler lives that match their values. One of the under-reported stories of our times is probably the number of women who have renounced the rat race and the "ladder of success" to raise their children and nurture their families. These are people who are discovering what is truly important to them, deciding on their priorities, and choosing to walk their own path ... "The [road] less traveled by," as Robert Frost observed in one of his best known poems, *The Road Not Taken.*

METAMORPHOSIS

At the beginning of this book, I described an insight into human nature: *everybody wants to be fulfilled.* I mentioned a guy who dreams about owning the corner gas station, a woman who desires a great career, and a young man who desires to be wealthy.

The reality is, those are the things they *think* will give them a sense of fulfillment. But when they walk their *Path of the Genie*, when they travel through the stations of humility and self-discovery, *their visions will change.* As Jesus said, "New wine cannot be kept in old wineskins." New understandings require new outlooks. New outlooks lead to new desires of the heart.

There is nothing wrong with what those three individuals wished for; but as they progress along the path, they will look beyond their initial goals to horizons that are more meaningful because they have a perspective they didn't have before. They will learn to see themselves and their world with new eyes, and fulfillment will take a new and different meaning ... something that will outlive them.

Just as a caterpillar in a magical process changes into a beautiful butterfly, so also *The Path of the Genie* becomes the process through which change occurs. As you change, your heart's desire changes with you. Then you discover that you are becoming the person you were meant to be.

Renowned trainer Tony Robbins states this very clearly: "Getting what you want is not the purpose of life ...

Getting what you want is not the purpose of life ... Getting what you want will not make you happy. What will make you incredibly happy is becoming the person you need to be.

Anthony Robbins

Getting what you want will not make you happy. What will make you incredibly happy is becoming the person you need to be."

IT'S YOUR TURN

Brush off the dust and grime of life's negatives like Aladdin did when he rubbed the lamp. Then you will hear the voice of your Genie within. Listen to his whisperings. Practice humility and enter the station of self-discovery.

119

As you discover yourself, you will appreciate yourself. Your comfort with yourself will allow you to forget self and focus on blessing others with your gifts. Then you will find yourself in the realm of self-offering. In self-offering, you will discover the meaning of freedom.

The heart's desire that you had at the beginning of your journey may have changed radically along the way, because you have been changing. Now you will see the world with new eyes and the world will look quite different. Another transformation will take place—the world will see you with new eyes too!

Discover and walk your *Path of the Genie*. May you attain your new heart's desire. Happy journeys.

The Path of the Genie

Dilip Ranjitha Abayasekara

The path of the Genie,
'Tis an old tale but true,
Yes, it's Aladdin's story,
But the path's made for you.

The first step is clear
It's to remove the grime
Hate, envy, and fear,
Drop them, and shine.

Your first wish – be humble,
To escape your cave,
Your strength you will double,
When other's gifts you do rave.

Your second wish – self-discovery,
To know who you are,
Unique gifts are the bowery,
That will take you afar.

Your third wish—self-offering,
That's giving of your self,
Make your life a true blessing,
You will live beyond self.

The path of the Genie,
Life's adventure for you,
You will enter the glory
Of fulfillment that's true.

ABOUT THE AUTHOR

Dilip Abayasekara is a professional speaker, trainer, and speech coach. His focus, through his training company, Speaker Services Unlimited, is to help people discover their own genius and find their path of fulfillment.

Dilip was born and raised in Colombo, Sri Lanka, where he attended Royal College. After moving to the USA, he graduated from Palm Beach College and then University of Florida (B.S., chemistry) after which he earned a Ph.D. in polymer and organic chemistry from Virginia Commonwealth University. After working for 12 years as an industrial scientist, he surrendered to his avocation—connecting, influencing, and enriching others through the power of the spoken word.

Dilip was twice a finalist at Toastmasters International's World Championship of Public Speaking, placing second in 1992. He is among a small number of Toastmasters who have received accreditation by Toastmasters International for professional level speaking skills. He is also a published poet. As of this writing, he is serving as the Senior Vice President of Toastmasters International.

Dr. Abayasekara also serves as Special Assistant to the President of Central Pennsylvania College.

"Dr. Dilip" has presented speeches and seminars in fifteen states in the USA and four other countries.

Dilip and his wife Sharon and children Allison and Alex reside in Camp Hill, Pennsylvania, USA.

SPEAKER SERVICES UNLIMITED

Speaker Services Unlimited helps individuals and organizations to think more creatively, speak more effectively, sell more persuasively, and lead more productively.

Keynote Speeches

The Path of the Genie...Your Journey to Your Heart's Desire
From a Strange Land to a Homeland: An Immigrant's Story
Life is an Elevator ... But You Push The Buttons
Winning at Life ... Lessons Learned at the Lectern

Customized Inspirational Keynotes for Your Organization

Workshops

- Communication Seminars & Workshops
- Leadership Seminars
- Creativity Workshops
- Sales Workshops
- Team Building Workshops
- Spirit-centered Workshops

Services for Speakers

- Professional and Executive Speech Coaching
- Individualized & Customized Voice Coaching
- Speech Evaluation Service
- Speechwriting Services

Contact Information

Website: www.drdilip.com
E-mail: drdilip@drdilip.com
Telephone: (717) 728-2203
SSU Enterprises
P.O. Box 405
Enola, PA 17025
USA

NAME INDEX